AN APOSTLE'S INNER LIFE

An Apostle's Inner Life

ANDREW MURRAY

Pickering & Inglis Ltd
Marshall Pickering
34–42 Cleveland Street, London, W1P 5FB, U.K.

First published in book form in 1989
by Pickering & Inglis Ltd
Part of the Marshall Pickering Holdings Group

Clarion Classics are published by the Zondervan Publishing House 1415 Lake Drive, S.E., Grand Rapids, Michigan 49506

British Library CIP Data

Murray, Andrew, *1828–1917*
An apostle's inner life

I. Title II. Series
225.9′24

ISBN 0–551–01866–6 (Marshalls)
0–310–56132–9 (Zondervan)

Text set in 10/11pt Times Roman by Watermark, Hampermill Cottage, Watford. Printed by Richard Clay Ltd, Bungay, Suffolk.

CONTENTS

Chapter 1

Paul an Example

'Howbeit for this cause I obtained mercy, that in me first Jesus Christ might shew forth all long-suffering, for a pattern to them which should hereafter believe on him to life everlasting.' 1 Timothy 1:16

How much Paul meant what he writes here, that Christ intended him to be a pattern for all believers, is seen in the confidence with which he so often appeals to the churches to imitate him. To the Thessalonians he writes: 'Yourselves know how ye ought to follow us: ... to make ourselves an ensample unto you to follow us' (2 Thess 3:7,9). To the Corinthians he says: 'Be ye imitators of me, even as I also am of Christ.' And to the Philippians: 'Those things, which ye have both learned, and received, and heard, and seen in me, do: and the God of peace shall be with you (Phil 4:9). Christ meant that in him should be seen what the mighty power of grace could do, not only in the conversion of a persecutor and blasphemer, but in a life of faith and service in which there would be a complete response and yielding up of all to the will and power of another.

We read that in the old Egyptian monuments in one of the Pyramids, the units of weight and measure were so fixed in the king's chamber that they might be there as a standard of appeal for all time. And we are told that into the walls of the Houses of Parliament in London, the yard and foot have been so built in as to furnish a fixed standard of length. If Christ's purpose in Paul to make such a display of the mighty power of his grace as to be for all time a revelation of what he could and would do, and of what a man who was a sinner could be and do through him and for him. In Paul, Christ meant to build into his whole life and being, and into the whole framework of the Christianity of which he was to be the Apostle, the standard of true devotion to himself.

The question may be asked, Why, when Christ gave himself as our perfect example, and suffered just that he might be able to sympathise and succour us in following his footsteps, why should Paul also be given us as an example? The answer is simple. With all that there is blessed and encouraging in the example of our Lord, the feeling always arises that his divine nature and sinless perfection, to some extent, rob the command to follow in his footsteps, of its force. It was to meet this difficulty that Christ chose Paul to make him a pattern of what he could do for the chief of sinners, and for all who should, like him, believe unto eternal life.

'See that thou make all things according to the pattern shewed to thee in the mount.' These words hold good of every pattern of the divine life which God's grace gives us. They remind us of the danger of our forgetting or neglecting in everything to judge by the divine standard God has set up. They teach us the need of the illumination of the Holy Spirit, lest we unconsciously form human conceptions of divine things, and lose the sight and the blessing and the power which the true apprehension of the divine standard alone can give. It is when on the mount of worship and adoration we wait for the heavenly vision of the pattern that was set us by Christ, in Paul, that we shall not only turn to Scripture for the doctrine it teaches, or the commands it gives, but shall gather up into one great whole, all that Paul so simply and unconsciously reveals of his inner life, as a life hid with Christ in God, and claim it for ourselves. It needs time and patience and waiting on God, if we are really to know the heavenly life as it dwells in Christ, as it is lived out in Paul, as we are to be partakers of it.

Just think a moment of what is implied when Paul says, 'Christ liveth in me,' or, 'For me to live is Christ.' When our Lord came to this world, it was with a threefold purpose. First of all, that he might have a true and perfect human life to give up to the Father as a ransom for our sin. Then that he might, through death and resurrection, gain a life to be given to us, so that we, even as the grain of corn brings forth seed, with power again to reproduce itself, might, like him, live the heavenly life here on earth. And last of all, he ascended to heaven, that from there he might, moment by moment, live out his own life in the believer. The Christian life is a life in which Jesus Christ himself absolutely and increasingly lives, and in which the following of his example is nothing but the natural outcome of his presence within. The call is so high and holy, the surrender to Christ and the fellowship with him needs to be so entire and habitual; the faith that is needed makes such a demand on our whole life and being, that it is only by a divine power that such a life is possible. To meet us in our need, and to provide for every difficulty, Jesus Christ took Paul, made him a monument of his grace, and bids us look at him as the living embodiment of what he can work for one who trusts him, and waits to work in us.

The more we study Paul's life and writings, the more we shall see that the one characteristic of his religion is an intense, unceasing, whole-hearted attachment to

Jesus Christ. His life had become so bound up with Christ's, that what was true of Christ became true of him too. He could speak of himself as crucified with Christ; all his sufferings were the sufferings of Christ; in all his ministry he speaks and labours as one who is in Christ Jesus, and is conscious that Christ works mightily in him. And through it all he so mingles what Christ is to him, and what Christ will equally be to all his people, that in everything the inspiration of his faith wakens in us the assurance: What Christ did for him Christ will do for me.

How much the church of today needs to heed the call to make everything according to the pattern shown on the mount! And how it needs to wait for the Holy Spirit's teaching to give the true vision of what that pattern is. How ministers and all 'who labour in the Lord', need to test their work by that of Paul, and to find from him what the secret is of his unbounded dependence on Christ, and his unceasing experience of his presence and power! However feeble our attempt is to study Paul's life, let us undertake it with the firm resolve to imitate him to the full, and with confident assurance that he who gave him to us as a pattern, will delight in showing us by the Spirit all that it means, and working in us all that it promises.

Chapter 2

A Monument of Grace

'And the grace of our Lord was exceeding abundant with faith and love which is in Christ Jesus.' 1 Timothy 1:14

In the word 'grace', there are two shades of meaning which need to be carefully distinguished, and then combined. Sometimes Scripture speaks of grace, as that gracious disposition which shows itself in favour of the unworthy. In this sense we speak of it specially in connection with the justifying of the ungodly, and praise it as free, sovereign, and unconditional, the only cause of our salvation. At other times the chief thought is that gracious operation of the divine power which works in us effectually, enabling us to do all that God would have us to be in life and service. In this sense we speak of the exceeding abounding, ever active and increasing grace of God, enabling us to abound in every good work, and fitting each one according to his measure for his place in

God's kingdom here upon earth. If we would fully understand the mind of the Spirit, we must aim at uniting the two thoughts, and always trust God for the grace that not only pardons and accepts, but works in us each moment with its divine energy to will and to do what is well-pleasing to him.

In both senses Paul was a monument of grace. It was the exceeding abundance of God's grace that chose and saved him as a blasphemer and prosecutor, the chief of sinners, and made him the chief of the Apostles. And it was the exceeding abundance of that grace too that sanctified him, delivered him from the power of sin, and fitted him to live holy and blameless and unreproveable, and strengthened him with divine strength for all the work to which God had called him. 'The grace of our Lord was exceeding abundant with faith and love which is in Christ Jesus.'

In writing to the Corinthians (1 Cor 15:9,10) we see how Paul combines the two aspects, as he first speaks of his utter unworthiness to be an Apostle and then praises the grace that was not in vain, but enabled him to labour more abundantly than they all. 'By the grace of God I am what I am: and his grace which was bestowed upon me was not in vain; but I laboured more abundantly than they all: yet not I, but the grace of God which was with me.' Paul's whole heart was so under the impression that it was all free and sovereign grace that chose and fitted him to be an Apostle, and that enabled him day by day so to labour that he did more than others, that he does not hesitate to speak boldly of what he had done because he felt that there could not be the shadow of a thought of glorying in himself. It was all so markedly the grace of God alone – his alone was the glory. The knowledge of the grace of God is no light matter. Paul tells us what the school was in which he learned. It was during the years of his stay at Tarsus, where he had been favoured with unspeakable visions and revelations of heavenly things, that his Lord saw the danger of him being over exalted. He sent a thorn in the flesh, an angel of satan to buffet him. Paul prayed repeatedly for deliverance. He could not understand why the answer was not given, until Jesus appeared to him and said, 'My grace is sufficient for thee: for my strength is made perfect in weakness.' At once he undertood it all. He saw that grace takes charge of everything and wards off a danger he had not thought of. That grace comes specially to keep us humble, that God may have all the glory. That grace is strength for whatever work we have to do. That that strength is bestowed in the midst of weakness, that we may learn to be strong in faith and give glory to God. And therefore this was the last lesson which he learned to carry with him through all his weakness and necessities. 'Most gladly will I glory in my infirmities, that the power of Christ may rest upon me ... when I am weak, then am I strong.' In every difficulty and perplexity he found in the exceeding grace of our Lord the full provision for every need.

It was the intense reality of entire dependence upon grace and an ever growing experience of its sufficiency for every step of his path that enabled Paul to speak with such confidence to Christians. Listen to those wonderful words to the Corinthians (2 Cor 9:8): 'And God is able to make all grace abound toward you; that ye, always having all sufficiency in all things, may abound to every good work.' Just think what that means. The almighty power of God, able to make all grace abound in each of his children, so that they at all times in all things having all sufficiency of the grace they need, may abound to all good works. Read the words over again. Note that 'all' is five times repeated. Think of God's omnipotence, able to make grace so abounding that we may, just as God abounds towards us, abound before him in all good works. Can anyone receive a statement more full and all-embracing, covering every possible emergency? For all we need, for cleansing from sin and perfecting holiness, for all we need in the midst of trial and suffering, in the middle of daily labour or spiritual work, we may have the utmost confidence that in Christ's grace there is all-sufficient power to fit us for every good work, that his strength will be made perfect in our weakness. God is in very deed able to make all grace every moment of the day to abound in us, that we may indeed abound to every good work.

If we would learn like Paul to believe and rejoice in this riches of grace, let us learn from him what the secret is of such absolute confidence in the sufficiency of grace for every breath of our spiritual life. At the root of all lies the deep sense of utter unworthiness, impotence and nothingness, a willingness to give up every thought of our own wisdom or strength, and so to live a life of absolute and unceasing dependence on grace alone. To this must be added the confident and joyous assurance that Christ will, if we entrust ourselves to him, take and keep charge of the work of grace down to its minutest details. With this we shall go on to that childlike surrender to an unhesitating obedience which will be the sign that the Father and his child understand and trust each other. And so with each new morning; we shall yield ourselves for God to fulfil his great purpose in us, and show forth the exceeding riches of his grace. And if, at any time, doubt or fear arise, we shall just look at the pattern man Christ gave us in Paul, and believe that he was made a monument of the exceeding grace of God to encourage and strengthen every traveller in the way of life, to praise for what he did for him, and will most certainly do for us too. 'By grace ye are saved through faith'; as boundless as the grace is to work out our salvation each moment let our faith be to claim all that it waits to do for us.

Chapter 3

Christ Revealed in Me

'When it pleased God ... to reveal his Son in me, that I might preach him among the heathen.' Galatians 1:15,16

When God sent his Son into the world it was that in him the life that was in the Father might be manifested and communicated to sinful man. When God revealed the Son in Paul, it was that he, by a special manifestation of grace, might be a pattern of the life of the Son revealed fully in a human being. It was to show how completely Christ could identify himself with a human life, and enable a man to identify him with Christ. And this again was with the view to Paul's manifesting to other men, not only by his teaching, but also and very specially by his living, what the life is that God has prepared for each one of us in Christ Jesus. Let us think for a moment about each of these three points.

1. The terrible ruin of sin was that it robbed man of the

life of God. In restoring man God's great object was to make him again partaker of the divine life, with the power to live it out in daily life, in blessed fellowship with himself. Jesus said: 'I am come that they might have life, and that they might have it more abundantly. To this end more than one thing was needed. Christ came that he might be a model man, teaching us how the life of God could dwell in human nature, and how man could yield himself up to God and his will, and find his happiness in him. He came too that in that life of his in human nature, he might prepare a perfect sacrifice to be offered up to the Father in death. This was the only way in which man could be delivered from the dominion of sin, and be set free to live to God and his glory. And in his death he gave up his life, not only to God, but to us too. Even as the grain of corn lives again in all the seeds that come from it, so Christ died that he might set his life free to live itself over again in us, so that all its obedience and humility and love, might in very truth be found and seen in our human life. This is that Son of God, of whom Paul said, 'It pleased God to reveal his Son in me, that I might preach him among the heathen.'

2. When Christ came to make God and the divine life known to us, he did it as much by living as by his teaching. 'He that hath seen me hath seen the Father.' It was so with Paul too. God's revelation of Christ in him, Christ living in him, was his preparation and his power for preaching the Gospel to the Gentiles. We think and speak of the amazing influence Paul has had on Christian thought by his Epistles. God alone knows what the influence has been which his life has exerted, and would still exert if the church understood its meaning. When Paul speaks of the excellency of the power that is of God working in him, of the exceeding and abounding riches of God's grace, giving him the victory over sin in his own experience and in the souls with whom he dealt, of his being crucified with Christ to the world, and sharing with him the weakness of his death and the power of his resurrection – this life of Christ in Paul has scarcely taken that

hold of the church and especially of its ministers, which it was meant to have. The appeals that Paul makes to his sincerity, his blamelessness, his devotion, his sufferings, and the intensity of his love, his counting all things but loss for Christ's sake, are proofs that he at least, fully knew that God had revealed Christ in him, that he might be the embodiment of that life before the world and the church.

3. As the life of God was seen in Christ, and the life of Christ was seen in Paul, so the life of Paul was to be seen in his converts. To the Thessalonians he writes (1 Thess 1:5): 'Ye know what manner of men we were among you ... and ye became followers of us and of the Lord', and (2 Thess 3:7–9): 'Yourselves know how ye ought to follow us ... to make ourselves an ensample unto you to follow us.' And to the Corinthians (1 Cor 4:16): 'I have begotten you through the gospel. Wherefore I beseech you, be ye followers of me.' Also 1 Cor 11:1: 'Be ye followers of me, even as I also am of Christ.' And to the Philippians (3:17): 'Brethren, be followers together of me, and mark them which walk so as ye have us for an ensample;' (4:9): 'Those things, which ye have both learned, and received, and heard, and seen in me, do: and the God of peace shall be with you.' His whole life was a gospel, a proclamation of what the grace of God could do and was doing. Christ living in him was the secret of his life, the power of his mighty influence, to some a witness and an inspiration even more effectual than his teaching or writing.

'It pleased God to reveal his Son in me, that I might preach him among the heathen.' To all to whom the ministry of the Gospel is entrusted, the lesson is one of deep suggestion and heart-searching. It is not the orthodoxy of our creed, it is not even the correctness of our scriptural teaching, but it is the life of Christ Jesus in us that will work effectually, that will enable us to labour, striving according to his working, which worketh in us mightily. There is indeed a great need in the ministry of the Gospel, for a return to a simpler and a fuller faith in its teaching. But there is a still more urgent need for that power of the divine life which comes alone from the full and unceasing dependence on the mighty power of God, from the fellowship with Christ dwelling in us, keeping us hour by hour in contact with himself. To every minister and to every missionary, and to every worker, Paul is an example of what Christ can do in filling a life, through the power of the Holy Spirit, with his life, and enabling him to pass it on in power to those who hear him.

'It pleased God to reveal his Son in me, that I might preach him among the heathen.' In God, in Christ, in Paul, in all who would be imitators of Christ and of Paul, the life is everything. And in this life in us Christ can be everything only as he is revealed within us by the Father. In all our study of Paul's character and power as the pattern Apostle we shall fail to discover the deepest secret of his power unless we take time to realize fully that it is all rooted in this one thing – Christ revealed in me. And we shall be able to follow in his footsteps only as we yield ourselves in the confidence of faith to expect that the Father will himself reveal his son in us.

Chapter 4

It Pleased God

'It pleased God who called me by his grace, to reveal his Son in me.' Galatians 1:15,16

In studying what has been written about St Paul I have been struck by how much the element is lacking that is expresssed in the words: 'It pleased God'. There is such a fear of curtailing or neglecting the human development of Paul's character, and such a fascination in constructing a life that shall make clear to us the whole personality of the greatest teacher of Christianity, that there is hardly room left for giving God his place. The result is that we do not come under the full impression of the share God had in making Paul what he was. We thus not only get a one-sided view of Paul's life and experience, but in our desire to profit by his example and become his imitators, we lose sight of the true secret, both to him and to us, of spiritual power – the deep sense of our entire unceasing dependence, in life and work, on him 'who worketh all things after the counsel of his will.'

In all our study of human nature we have always to deal with the two great factors, God's sovereignty and man's liberty. They are so inextricably intertwined that it is hardly possible to express clearly and fully their mutual relationship. Our only safety is, with two apparently conflicting truths, to take each one separately, and yield ourselves to the full acknowledgement of its claims. We shall then be prepared, if not to find the secret of their perfect reconciliation, at all events, in practice to give each side of the truth its due.

There is another thing we have to remember. The student who is seeking to adjust the claims to two parties, himself belongs to one of them, and cannot help being one-sided. It needs true humility of spirit, a deep distrust of human wisdom, and the teachable surrender to the guidance of the Holy Spirit, if we are to do full justice to the claims of God. It is only in this way that the life in which God and man are co-workers will open to us the wonderful mystery of God working all in man and man working all in God. It is only thus that we shall be able to appreciate the light that is cast on all Paul's life by a single phrase like this, 'It pleased God'.

In realising fully how much in Paul's spiritual development was owing directly to God's intervention, let us above all cultivate the confident assurance that no one can be so jealous as God himself of giving full scope to the powers and the liberty which he has bestowed upon man. A wise Father or teacher is careful not to give a child more help than is absolutely needed, to enable him to think for himself. We may be sure that God will take much more care not to violate the laws he himself laid down for man's liberty. The deeper this conviction enters into us, the more ready we shall be to accept with confidence and with joy all that Paul meant when he said, 'It pleased God to reveal his Son in me.' And we shall be prepared for a deeper apprehension of the words, 'Christ revealed in me'; 'God revealed Christ in me'; 'It pleased God to reveal Christ in me.'

'Christ revealed in me': Paul speaks of what God had wrought in him as the very centre and essence of his preaching to the Gentiles. 'I am made a minister,' he says to the Colossians (1:25–27): 'to fulfil the word of God ... to make known what is the riches of the glory of this mystery among the Gentiles; which is Christ in you, the hope of glory.' And where he writes to the Ephesians concerning the mystery of Christ to be preached to the Gentiles (Eph 3:16,17), he adds the prayer 'That God would grant you ... to be strengthened with might by his Spirit in the inner man; That Christ may dwell in your hearts through faith.' To the Corinthians (2 Cor 13:3) he says 'Ye seek a proof of Christ speaking in me, which to you-ward is not weak, but is mighty in you.' So also to the Galatians, after having spoken of himself, 'Christ liveth in me,' he says, 'I travail in birth again until Christ be formed in you' (4:19). He was possessed by the one thought that Christ lived and spoke and wrought through him – 'He was mighty in me towards the Gentiles.' And he meant them to understand that nothing less could satisfy him than that they too should be partakers of this grace. What God had done for him he would do for them.

'God revealed his Son in me.' It was not by his own effort, it was through his own faith, that he received this indwelling Christ, but through a direct intervention of omnipotent power. We find in the farewell discourse (John 14:15–23) that, in connection with the coming of the Holy Spirit, Christ promised, 'At that day ye shall know that ye are in me, and I in you.' 'If a man love me my Father will love him, and we will come and make our abode with him.' Christ meant this to be the privilege and the characteristic mark of every whole-hearted disciple. God made Paul partaker of it. Paul lived in the full, and, as far as we can discover from his writings, the unbroken enjoyment of it. Out of this life he preached it as his gospel in the power of the Holy Spirit. How little the church of our day understands and claims and experiences such a promise, or knows how to lead believers to its attainment. We need to return to the place Abraham occupied, to believe in 'God Almighty' as he did, to bow before him in deep reverence and dependence, and to receive this life of Christ in us directly from himself, who calleth the things that are not, as though they were. God will still do for us what he did for Paul.

'It pleased God to reveal his Son in me.' The initiative was with God. And so too the daily power that secured the continuance and perfection of the work. It was all the free, sovereign, and omnipotent grace of God, 'The Father, of whom are all things': 'The same God which worketh all in all.' We shall find in our study of Paul how unceasingly he falls back upon the thought that he owes everything to God, and loves to acknowledge his absolute and continual dependence on him for every movement of his inner life. The more we cultivate this disposition and feel how it is only by the direct intervention of the divine will that the wonderful manifestation of himself and the Father which Christ promised, the more shall we be brought low under a sense of our nothingness, and be fitted for receiving the wonderful gift of Christ actually and unceasingly dwelling in us.

In these words of Paul we have the key that will open to us the way of that low spiritual state which marks so much of the Christian life. 'Christ revealed in me'; that must not be a spiritual luxury, a mystic enjoyment, but the natural outcome of a life entirely given up into God's hands, for him to work out his own purpose in us. So alone can we be fitted fully to preach the Gospel to the Gentiles. 'Christ in you the hope of glory.' Where the almighty power of God is looked for and confidently expected, God will prove that he is faithful to his promise in our personal experience and in our service for the kingdom.

'It pleased God'! Until this, the innermost secret of the inner life of Paul, takes the place it is meant to have in our theology, in our life, in all our teaching – until God has his honour as God of whom are all things – the church will never reach the level to which God sent his Son, and sent his servant Paul, too, to invite her.

Chapter 5

The Chief of Sinners

'This is a faithful saying, and worthy of all acceptation, that Christ Jesus came into the world to save sinners; of whom I am chief.'
1 Timothy 1:15

Paul had spoken (1 Tim 1:11–14) of the exceeding grace God had manifested, not only in his conversion, but in his being put into the ministry, and the grace that enabled him faithfully to fulfil it. In our text he proceeds to give in one sentence the sum of his Gospel – Jesus Christ came into the world to save sinners – and points to himself as a witness to its truth and power. He was a sinner, a sinner whom Christ had saved, a chief of sinners.

A Sinner. Not only a man who has sometimes committed sin, but one who was so under its power that his nature was wholly evil. A nature so blinded by sin, that while thinking he was doing God service, he was rejecting the righteousness of God, and was even a persecutor of God's church, and of God's Son himself. A sinner – the word suggests what a discovery it must have been to Saul, who had always spoken of 'sinners of the Gentiles,' to find what it meant to himself to be in terrible reality a sinner before God. It was in this struggle that for three days he neither ate nor drank; a death struggle to give up his name and his righteousness as a Pharisee, and to consent to be a sinner, saved by sovereign grace.

A saved sinner. After having preached the Gospel for nearly thirty years, Paul here acknowledges that he had himself to accept salvation on the same terms on which he had offered it to the darkest and most degraded heathen. We think, in connection with the conversion of Saul, of the wonderful revelation of the living Lord Jesus in heaven, as entering into his heart, now to become his life, and of his calling to be the Apostle of the Gentiles. But we forget what we learn from Paul in these words, that all was comprised in the one word – 'Christ Jesus came into the world to save sinners.' 'God exalted Christ to give repentance and remission of sins;' it was this salvation the vision of the exalted Lord brought him. And throughout the whole of his life and ministry these two words constitute the essence of his Gospel – 'Christ Jesus came to save sinners.' In this lay his power, he lived and he preached as a saved sinner. The grace of God which came to him was so wonderful, the salvation which he found and enjoyed was so complete, the love of God in Christ to everyone who is content to be nothing less and nothing else but a sinner, was so inconceivably blessed, that he could not for a moment live in any other atmosphere but that of the adoring exclamation – A saved sinner!

In all this the Christian graces had their root. It kept him in the place of boundless humility. It taught him even when he had to vindicate his place as 'in nothing behind the very chiefest apostle,' still to say, 'though I be nothing,' as one who had so accepted his death in Christ the crucified, he could literally say. 'I live no longer.' It bound him in absolute surrender to live every moment dependent upon his Lord, and it kept him in the confidence and joy that Christ himself would keep him to the very end.

The chief of sinners. When Christ apprehended Saul in the very height of his life of persecution and blasphemy there came to him such a sense of the awfulness of his sin, that he never through life could think of himself otherwise than as the greatest sinner of all. Of no man's sin could he ever have such a conception as God's light from heaven had given him of his own. It was this that fitted him for being an example to all who should believe. This made him capable of yielding himself absolutely and entirely for the grace of God to master and to sanctify wholly. Never for one moment, in the midst of his most exultant faith and joyous thanksgiving, was that deep undertone missing – the chief of sinners. He carried it with him to heaven. In its worship the deepest humiliation will be the height of blessedness, as we sing, 'A sinner saved by grace.'

When God revealed himself to Job in his omnipotence, he cried out, 'I abhor myself.' When Isaiah saw the Lord, as the seraph proclaimed his holiness, he cried out, 'Woe is me, I am undone.' When Saul saw that same Lord in his wonderful grace, as the crucified and glorified one, he so felt his sin that he remained three days speechless. In the holy light of that vision the true nature of sin was revealed as ungodliness, as enmity to God, rejecting and defying him. And in the prayer which he offered, 'God be merciful to me, a sinner,' there was burnt into his inmost being what it means to be a saved sinner. Nothing can reveal sin so effectually and so abidingly as the grace of God showing forth the exceeding riches. It teaches a man to say, 'A chief of sinners.'

But what now about the sins of his life after conversion? Many have quoted this text as if Paul had meant these too. 'It is not', they say, 'in the daily, or the occasional sins, into which Paul must have fallen, that he feels himself the chief of sinners too?' If we study the connection, both here and in 1 Cor 15:9,10, we shall see that the reference is entirely to his life as a blasphemer and persecutor. And as we look elsewhere in his writings, to find what he thinks of the sins of his regenerate state, we shall be surprised to see how little there is that Paul has to say about them. Nowhere do we find in him anything like confession of sin into which he has fallen. He speaks of the flesh, and its evil nature, as still present, with its temptations, calling for watchfulness and decision. But he ever speaks at the same time of the Spirit of life in Christ Jesus as makng him free from the law of sin and death. He ever boasts in Christ the Lord, 'who guards him from evil,' who dwells and works within, and fits him for a life with every thought brought 'into captivity to the obedience of Christ' (2 Cor 10:5).

To some this thought may be new. Let us with an unprejudiced mind study the Epistles one by one, and see whether we find any definite acknowledgement of sin, either committed or allowed in the heart. When once we are sure of what Paul says, we may have the opportunity in our further study of his life to examine the meaning of the attitude he takes.

It has been said of the Rev Charles Fox by one who knew him well, that there was such an intense sense of God in him that the call to humiliation constant and abiding was never for a moment absent. Confession not only meant the telling out of individual and separate sin, but was an attitude of heart in which the thought was never absent, that nothing of good is owing to ourselves, and in which, therefore, in childlike confidence, everything is always ascribed to the wonderful grace of God. Even in heaven this tone of confession will be recognised in every song of praise – 'To him that loved us, and washed us from our sins in his own blood.'

The remark has been made that there was no reason why Paul should make such confession, and not keep it secret between himself and his God. If there be any truth in this, it suggests the question why Paul is so little copied in this. Or, is the lack of confession of separate sins simply owing to the fact that God, who had so wonderfully created him anew, by a special power of grace kept him from sinning? Or does it mean that the grace of God is indeed ready to keep all who yield themselves utterly to the power of Christ's life and death in them, and by the power of his Holy Spirit to make free from the power of the flesh? The study of Paul's inner life

Chapter 6

Saul the Pharisee

'As touching the law, a Pharisee ... touching the righteousness which is in the law, blameless.' Philippians 3:5,6

In visiting a paper factory or a pottery special interest is always felt in noticing the unlikely material from which such pure and beautiful results are attained. In studying the life of Paul we can only fully realise the grace of God, when we think of what he was, and what God made of him. With all the servants of God in the Old and New Testament, patriarchs and kings, prophets and apostles, we see God ordinarily using men in whom there appeared to be some measure of readiness for his service. But to this rule Paul was a striking exception. As a Pharisee he was the embodiment of that self-righteousness which boasted in the law, while it was utterly ignorant of, and refused submission to, the righteousness of God. He was a type of Israel, in its departure from God, and everything like spiritual worship. He was the incarnation of that bitter hostility to Jesus which had crucified him, and now sought to destroy everyone who professed his name.

Saul the Pharisee, just because he believed so intensely in the law, and lived for it, became Saul the persecutor. He tells us himself that he blasphemed the name of Jesus and compelled others to blaspheme. To know this Pharisee, blasphemer and persecutor, will prepare us for adoring the wisdom of God in taking a man who had done his utmost to fulfil the law and to root out the name of Jesus from the earth, and make him a preacher of the righteousness of faith, and a witness that Jesus is Lord and Christ.

In the time of Christ we find three classes of Pharisee. The large majority belonged to those whom Christ denounced as appearing outwardly righteous before men, 'but within ye are full of hypocrisy and iniquity.' On the other side there were a few like Nicodemus and Joseph in whom the law had done its work of rousing a sense of sin and preparing the heart for receiving Christ. In between these there were men like Gamaliel, who honestly sought to keep the commandments of the law, and so to secure the divine favour. To this latter class Paul belonged. He says in 2 Timothy 1:3, 'I thank God, whom I serve from my forefathers with pure conscience.' He writes (Gal 1:14), 'I profited in the Jews' religion above many ... being more exceedingly zealous of the traditions of my fathers.' His life appears to have been an honest, whole-hearted devotion to the service of God, through the law, as he had been taught to know and keep it. With all the intensity of his nature, he had yielded his whole life and every moment of it,to the rule of the law; in it he trusted for his acceptance with God; in it he hoped for the fulfilment of all God's promises to Israel in the coming kingdom of glory.

The question arises: How was it possible that a man like Saul, and with him practically all other people, could be so deceived in their judgment of the law? It will be of importance to us to answer this question. We find in Scripture that there are two aspects under which the law is spoken of. It was to serve a double purpose. The one was to give the knowledge of God's holy will, and to show what was needed to please him. The other was to bring man to a consciousness of his own sinfulness, and his impotence to keep that law, and so to show him his need of God's grace both for the pardon of his sin, and the power for obedience. The former aspect one finds in the promises given by God, through Moses of the blessing which the keeping of the law would bring. In the book of Psalms, from the first to the 119th, with its praise for God's statutes, its confession of impotence to keep them aright, its unceasing prayer for divine teaching and divine enabling for their fulfilment, one finds continual testimony to the blessedness and the power of the law of God. The other aspect one finds in Moses too, where he speaks of the disobedience of Israel, and the great judgments that would come upon it. The history of Israel is a terrible proof of how little the law was able to create a spirit of obedience. Law is always meant to curb and check a spirit that is inclined to evil. In the sacrificial ritual of Moses, with its expiation of sin and promise of pardon and restoration, God showed how impossible it was for anyone to find his righteousness in the law. The law was meant to lead and help men in the path of obedience. But it was also meant to show what they could not do, and so bring them in penitence to seek their righteousness, not in the law, but in the mercy of God.

And how was it that Israel had so entirely misunderstood the meaning and the blessing of the law? It was because of the hardness of their hearts. This is the great point that comes out in Stephen's address when he had been accused of speaking blasphemous words against the law. He charged the Jews, to whom he spake, with having done what their fathers all along did. The evil nature had been seen in the patriarchs when 'they, moved with envy,' sold Joseph into Egypt; in the people when Moses thought they would deliver them, 'but they understood not', and said, 'Who made thee a ruler and a judge over us?' When Moses received the law, they would not obey him, and God gave them up to worship the host of heaven. They killed the prophets, and became the murderers of the Just One. Stephen sums up all, 'Ye stiffnecked and uncircumcised ... ye do always resist the Holy Ghost: as your Fathers did, so do ye.'

Their utterly worldly nature was not only the cause of disobedience but of something more terrible; they had lost the power of apprehending the holy and spiritual nature of the law. They rested content in external observances, and counted them their righteousness. Instead of allowing themselves, by the law, to be brought to God and his grace, the law became a veil to hide God from them. They rested content with their human appreciation and fulfilment of the law, and became utterly estranged from the true God. Such was Paul, too, when he was apprehended of Christ.

In the parable of the Pharisee and Publican Christ gives a striking illustration of the two aspects of the law and the work it does. In the Pharisee we see the religion of man; God must listen to hear how good he is. In the Publican we have the religion of God; man as a transgressor of the law calling upon God for his mercy. The parable points to the wonderful process needed, by which the proud Pharisee, rejoicing in his righteousness, becomes the penitent Publican truly justified and praising God for his mercy.

What Paul later wrote of the heathen was true of the Jews also, 'They changed the truth of God for a lie, and worshipped the creature rather than the Creator.' The truth of God's law was changed into a lie, and men worshipped themselves more than the Creator. That lie, inherent in all religion that puts its trust in the law, is the delusion that the law can be fulfilled. This is the religion of the natural man. It was this led, so soon after the death of Paul, in the church, to a return both in ritual and doctrine, to carnal observances and confidences. It is this that, even in the churches of the Reformation, still poisons the Christian life and keeps earnest and honest souls in bondage. It hinders them from understanding what the Gospel is that Paul preached, of being dead to the law, and of standing in that wonderful liberty wherewith Christ has made us free. God grant that as we study Paul we may find out how God chose him, the proudest of the Pharisees, that he might teach us from his own experience, how the law can bring nothing but a curse, and how Christ can give us, by his presence and life and love, that law written in the heart, in which there is perfect peace and blessedness.

Chapter 7

Christ Apprehending Paul

'As he journeyed, he came near Damascus: and suddenly there shined round about him a light from heaven: And he fell to the earth, and heard a voice saying unto him, Saul, Saul, why persecutest thou me? And he said, Who art thou, Lord? And the Lord said, I am Jesus whom thou persecutest.' Acts 9:3–5

In studying the conversion of Paul, we need specially to note how much there is in it of the supernatural. We shall see this in four particulars. A supernatural fact as the foundation of the new life he receives – the crucified Jesus glorified in heaven.

A supernatural revelation in the light from heaven shining into his heart. A supernatual power changing his whole being. A supernatural life and work as the outcome of the wonderful change. All was comprised in the one great act of God's revealing Christ in Paul's life and heart. What that must have meant we shall discover by comparing it with the manifestation of the risen Christ to his disciples.

When our Lord spoke of his coming death, he said, 'Yet a little while, and the world seeth me no more; but ye see me: because I live, ye shall live also.' They were to have the privilege of seeing him in the glory – power of his new life, in which he was to live in God's glory. According to the measure of love and faith, he manifested himself at different times. But in the words he spoke to Thomas, 'Because thou hast seen me, thou hast believed: blessed are they that have not seen, and yet have believed,' he gave his disciples for all ages the assurance that faith could be to them all that sight had been to the eleven. From heaven he would as the exalted one manifest himself so that we should lack nothing of the blessing of personal vision.

And yet it pleased God to make Paul partaker by the heavenly vision of a manifestation of Christ that should be for his lifetime, the possession of an abiding personal presence. He was thus to be fitted to be a witness to the great mystery to be preacher to the Gentiles, 'Christ in you, the hope of glory'; its witness and the exponent of it to the church throughout all the ages. The vision of Christ was not only to give him the rank of an Apostle, but to give him that enduement of power by which he was to be fitted for carrying about the living Christ speaking through him, and imparting himself in like manner to others. This is the unique place that Paul has to occupy in the church, the inconceivable privilege of being the one man to whom, in a light above the brightness of the sun, turning the natural light and his vision of it into utter darkness, the exalted Christ in his divine glory at the right hand of the power of God, made himself personally known. All Paul's life, all the mighty power he exerted through the whole Roman Empire, all the influence that he still exerts, is the proof of its divine reality.

We have already seen what the material was out of

which Christ was to make his chosen vessel – the proud Pharisee with his blameless righteousness and his zeal for God and his law persecuting the church. We have seen the Lord; the exalted Lord is prepared to lay hold of this man, and to work in him the mightiest transformation that he ever wrought. Let us listen to the story. As Paul was on his way to Damascus, 'breathing out threatenings and slaughter against the disciples, being exceedingly mad against them,' he draws near to Damascus ready to prove his zeal for God in blaspheming the name of the crucified Jesus, and compelling others to blaspheme. All at once, the light of the divine glory shines upon him. As if thunderstruck, he falls to the earth. He hears a voice, 'Saul, Saul, why persecutest thou me?' In amazement he cries, 'Who art thou, Lord?' Twice over he has heard the words, 'thou persecutest me.' It could be none other than Jesus himself, the crucified one, identifying himself with his disciples. What the Christians had said about Jesus, that he was risen and exalted to the right hand of God, is then indeed true.

The words that Christ added (Acts 26:14) 'It is hard for thee to kick against the pricks,' revealed to Paul that this divine being has been watching all that has been going on in his heart. In a voice of mingled compassion and entreaty, he reminds him how hopeless resistance has been. The word shows us that Paul has been struggling against the voice of conscience, and against God himself. The part he had taken in the disputes with Stephen, when in the synagogues of Cicilia and Asia (Acts 6:9,10), 'They were not able to resist the wisdom and the spirit by which he spake,' the power in which Stephen had spoken the words that led to his death, and charged them with being as their Fathers, stiffnecked and uncircumcised in heart and ears, the vision in which all that sat in Council 'saw his face as it had been the face of an angel,' must have made such an impression on him as to raise the question whether their witness was not the truth. When Paul answered (Acts 22:10), 'What shall I do, Lord?' he yielded himself without reserve to him who had laid hands on him. No one could then have imagined how completely this was the end of all resistance, what a final and eternal surrender to a life in which he was to have no will, but that of the Lord who had conquered him. At the command, 'Arise, and go into Damascus; and there it shall be told thee of all things which are appointed for thee to do,' he went forward to a path of devotion and suffering which never ended until he met his Lord in that heaven from which he had heard him speak.

When our Lord appeared to Ananias and gave him the commission to tell Saul what his work was to be, he summed up what he thought of Paul in the words, 'behold he prayeth.' As a Pharisee, Paul had prayed much and often. As a sinner, never. For the first time brought into the presence of Christ and of God, made conscious of his terrible sin, fully assured that the power that had stopped him in his career, and made itself master of his whole being, was that of an infinite mercy, he learnt what prayer truly is, the response of a broken heart to the infinite love of God. That prayer with its question, 'What shall I do, Lord?' was the proof that he had indeed passed from death unto life. The study of the three days that he spent at Damascus blind and dumb will show us something of what prayer must have been.

Chapter 8

Paul Apprehending Christ

'They led Paul by the hand, and brought him into Damascus. And he was there three days without sight, and neither did eat nor drink.'
Acts 9:8,9

Christ's apprehending Paul was the act of a moment, complete and immediate. Paul's apprehending of Christ began at the same moment but was continued throughout life, so that in old age he could say, 'Not as though I had already attained ... but I follow after, if that I may apprehend.'

It is a point of the utmost importance to observe that Paul knows nothing of any progressive stages or gradual progress in his conversion to the Gospel. He looked back to it throughout his life as a sudden overwhelming event, which surprised him in the full tide of his Judaic career, and drove him, in spite of himself, into a new channel. He is a conquered rebel, whom God leads in triumph in the face of the world (2 Cor 2:14). If he preaches the Gospel he cannot make any boast of doing so; he was compelled to preach it, under a higher necessity, which he had no power to resist. There he stands – a slave in chains (1 Cor 9:15–18).

'His conversion was the fruit of God's grace, manifesting itself in him as a sovereign power which triumphed over his individual will. Paul rose from the ground the captive of that divine grace to which he henceforth was to render himself without reserve or condition.' (Sabatier, pp 62,68.)

These words are strong but true. Paul had done his utmost to resist the power of Christ and his truth. The revelation on the way to Damascus overwhelmed and over-mastered him. He was led into the city a prisoner of Jesus Christ. He had surrendered at discretion; during the three following days he could do nothing but bow in speechlesss amazement at the terrible sin that he had been guilty of, and the inconceivable grace that had been bestowed upon him.

No human thought can conceive or describe what must have passed through his mind as he felt himself face to face with the crucified Jesus on the throne of glory. 'Is this', he must have thought, 'what all my boasted blamelessnesss in the law has brought me to. I have been found fighting against God himself, crucifying the Son of God afresh.' He had used the law as a pedestal on which to exalt himself and be crowned with the divine favour. And all at once he sees that his righteousness has become his condemnation. He feels that as blasphemer of the name of Jesus Christ, and the persecutor of his church, he is the chief of sinners. Never man had thus sinned; never man had thus seen his sin in the light of God from heaven.

Saul fell down dead at the feet of Jesus. It is only when we realise the terrible reality of that death to all his hopes and self-confidence, that we can form any idea of the intensity of that new life on which he entered. In him the experience of the prophet Jonah was repeated.

Christ had said that no sign should be given to the Jews but that of Jonah. Jonah was the only prophet ever sent on a direct mission to the Gentiles. He had, like all the nations, so little sympathy with God's purpose, that to escape his mission he fled. The experiences he passed through 'in the belly of hell' were to him nothing less than death. As the result he gave himself to fulfil his calling, and yet still proved how little the Spirit of God and his compassion had mastered him. The old covenant could not work anything but an eternal submission. In Jesus Christ the sign of Jonah had its fulfilment. He whom the Father had sent had to spend three days in the grace to prove that it is only through an entire death to the life of nature that the divine glory could enable a man to give his life for the world and the lost, and in the power of heaven to carry out God's purpose of love. Saul had been chosen of God as the Apostle of the Gentiles. In the revelation of Christ, the sign of the prophet Jonah was fulfilled in him too as he was brought into that new world which opened by death and resurrection of our Lord. These three days spent as in the silence of the grave, were his death to the law, to sin, to self, and all its effort. All was summed up in the one word, 'God be merciful to me a sinner.' The proud Pharisee died; the penitent publican rose from his grave, a prepared vessel to carry the message of God's love to the Gentile world.

Amid all the sense of sin and shame, Saul felt that it was infinite grace that Christ had met him as the Saviour of sinners. The vision of the heavenly Christ carried with it the power of his presence as exalted by God to give repentance and remission of sins. The mingled sense of abounding sin and abounding grace, which constituted a chief element of the blessedness of heaven, had come to him.

When Ananias came to him his inmost soul was prepared to receive his message. The work that Christ himself had begun from heaven is continued and completed through a man in the flesh. Saul is to be linked as closely to the body of Jesus on earth as to the head in heaven.

Through Ananias he receives his sight, a pledge that God who said 'Let there by light,' had shined into his heart the light of the knowledge of the glory of God in the face of Christ Jesus.

Through Ananias he received in baptism the washing away of his sins. Many years later he wrote, 'We were baptized into his death' (Rom 6:3, 'Buried with Christ in baptism, wherein ye are risen with him' (Col 2:12). 'For by one Spirit are we all baptized into one body' (1 Cor 12:13). Paul wrote to Christians from among the heathen in the confident expectation that the Holy Spirit would teach them to understand the reality of their union with Christ in his death and resurrection. During his three days of darkness, Saul had indeed passed through the pains of death; by faith in the risen Lord, who had manifested himself to him in the power of a divine life, Saul knew the power of his resurrection. It was to him the beginning and the power of the eternal life. Of its meaning he was to learn more in the future, a life in which Christ was put on and he became one plant with him in the likeness of his death, and in the likeness of his resurrection too. When Jesus the crucified and risen Lord took possession of him he became partaker of the divine reality, for which, in later years, he found the thought and words.

'That thou mayest be filled with the Holy Ghost.' Christ from heaven had opened and prepared the heart; what a deep mystery that his servant on earth should be the instrument for conveying that Holy Spirit which Christ had sent down from his throne of power. It was the very Spirit of Pentecost that was to come upon Saul and make him a member of Christ's body upon earth, dependent upon those to whom he is now united. Saul did not know what Christ had promised the disciples in connection with the gift of the Holy Spirit. 'He shall reveal me'; 'He shall glorify me'; 'He shall guide you into all truth'; 'He shall testify of me'; and 'Ye also shall bear witness'. But all that those words implied became his very own, when in a heart broken and truly opened up by the heavenly vision, he received the Spirit to reveal the Christ who now lived within him. There is no higher expression for the work of the Pentecostal Spirit than this, that he makes Christ such a living reality that a man can truly say, 'Christ liveth in me.'

In the words of our Lord to Ananias with regard to Saul, 'Behold he prayeth,' we find the divine expression for what Saul's conversion really meant. As a Pharisee he had prayed unceasingly; it was part of that blamelessness in the law in which he put his trust. And yet he had never prayed in truth. The heavenly vision brought him for the first time to bow before God in that sense of deep and entire dependence upon him which constitutes the very essence of prayer. And it revealed to him the greatness of the sin in which he had lived, and from which he saw that nothing but divine mercy could free him. How truly that prayer became the spirit and the attitude of his whole future life, his Epistles abundantly testify. In all his understanding of Christ he always found in him the access to the Father in which all that fullness of the divine life could manifest itself in the feebleness of human nature. He that would understand the inner life of St Paul must above all learn to know the place that prayer took in his life.

Chapter 9

A Chosen Vessel

'For he is a chosen vessel unto me, to bear my name before the Gentiles, and kings, and the children of Israel.' Acts 9:15

The history of the human race is often regarded as an unconscious evolution in which, just as a tree grows out of its seed, the men who influence the world make their appearance according to laws that to us are utterly unknown. Scripture gives us an entirely different view. It speaks of Pharaoh and Cyrus and others as 'men raised up by God' for his own special purpose. This is more particularly the case with all the men needed at the great critical periods of the history of God's church. And it is of none more true than of Saul, when our Lord said to Ananias, 'He is a chosen vessel unto me.' In the counsels of eternity he had been selected and set apart for a work in some respects greater than any that had yet been entrusted to man.

The kingdom of God, which had hitherto been given into the keeping of the Jewish nation, was now to pass from them to the great Gentile world. A mystery which had been kept a secret throughout the ages was now to be revealed and fulfilled. It was to work such a revolution in the spiritual world, and to have such far-reaching consequences in the history of mankind, that only a man of special gift and power, under the influence of an extraordinary intervention of divine grace, could accomplish the work.

1. Saul was to be, first of all, the Apostle of the Gentiles. Christ had chosen twelve Apostles to whom the charge of the church, as it was to be seen among the Jews, was committed. To Saul the whole Roman world was entrusted. A man of extraordinary gifts, of mind, of will, and of heart, born to be a leader of men, with a power for daring and doing and enduring such as few men had possessed, God found in him what he needed. He was able to take the oversight of the millions given into his charge. The force of his intellect fitted him to be the chief teacher the world has ever seen, and down through the centuries his words still attract more attention and exercise a mightier influence than those of any man who has ever lived. As God had chosen him, and endued him with all the requisite powers, he fulfilled his commission with a devotion, an intensity and success that proved the wisdom of the divine choice. The churches of Christendom today, with all they are doing for the heathen world, are the living witnesses that the truth as received from Paul has indeed power to elevate and to save. The great message that the Gentiles are fellow-heirs and of the household of God is the Gospel that alone gives hope to the world.

2. But Saul had a larger and still more difficult task. The Christians from among the Jews could not understand what appeared to them would be unfaithfulness on the part of God, that the Gentiles should not only have admission to the church which Christ had established among God's ancient people, but that Israel should now

be rejected and cast off and the kingdom pass over to the Gentile nations. The Apostles of our Lord could hardly take it in, and they were powerless to secure the approval of the Jewish Christians. Saul was the chosen vessel to vindicate the righteousness of God in his dealings with the nations. What we find taught in Romans chapters 9–11 is but the expression of what Paul in his fellowship with the Apostles had maintained as the will of God. To his own mind it had been a painful struggle that cost him tears, to see that the nation had finally rejected Christ, and that there was now but a small remnant returning to acknowledge him as Lord. Even where he was opposed and misrepresented and had to stand alone he fought the battle for truth, and succeeded in bringing Jews and Gentiles to accept the mystery and trust him to make clear what was so dark.

3. In this connection he had to bring out the great truth of the Body of Christ. The contempt and hatred with which the Jew had for centuries looked down upon the heathen, the enmity and distrust with which the Gentiles had regarded and often persecuted the Jews, had all been done away with at the cross of Christ. There he had slain the enmity and created of those two, one new man, making peace. In Christ Jesus there was now to be no longer Jew or Gentile; Christ was all and in all. In his own person Paul exemplified the truth he taught. He could wish himself accursed for the sake of his brethren after the flesh. And yet, with his passionate love for his people, he gave his whole being in an intensity of devotion for the Gentiles that for long years made him die daily for them. It is owing to Paul's teaching that the new church, with such diverse elements indeed, became one Body in Christ.

4. There was much more than this for which Paul, the chosen vessel, had been set apart. The Apostles and other disciples among the Jews had been brought to Christ and to Pentecost and to the membership of the kingdom of heaven, without having to give up their connection with the law of Moses. It appeared to them most

natural that the Gentiles should enter the church by an act of submission to that same law. Was it not in very deed the law of God, holy and good and righteous? To Paul the task was entrusted by God to secure the liberty of the Gentiles from the bondage of the law. It was given to him to get an insight into what the law truly meant. 'By the law is the knowledge of sin'; 'The law worketh wrath'; 'As many as are of the works of the law are under the curse.' In words such as these, he taught what no one else had hitherto understood, but what God had revealed to him, that the great object of the law was to bring man to a sense of his impotence and to the experience that the law in itself could bring him nothing but a curse. There could be no thought of any righteousness of the law; that meant, that righteousness could come from God alone by faith; no justification by the works of the law; a full and everlasting justification through the righteousness of God in Christ; this was Paul's gospel.

5. In contrast to the law Paul places the promise, the Spirit, Christ himself, and faith, as the power of the new life of the believer. In Galatians and Romans he shows how righteousness of God by faith is manifested in the new and divine life of Christ through the Holy Spirit dwelling in us. The true and full liberty from the law can only be found in 'the law of the Spirit of life in Christ Jesus.' 'That the righteousness of the law might be fulfilled in us, who walk in the Spirit.' Even where the church has accepted Paul's great doctrine of justification by faith, she is still only learning what its blessed result is to be – a life in union with the crucified and risen Christ, a life of which nothing less must be known than this – 'Christ liveth in me.'

6. 'He is a chosen vessel unto me, to bear my name before the Gentiles, and kings, and the children of Israel.' This is the sphere of labour to which Paul was ordained by Christ. He was to bear his name, not only in testimony and teaching, but in the power of a life in which it pleased God himself to reveal the Son in him. He was to be a man, so bearing the likeness of Christ in

his sufferings and death, in his life and power, that even as Christ, he too gave his life for the world.

Paul is still the chosen vessel, revealing Christ to the church and the world as no other man has done it. When the church returns to acknowledge him, not only as the great preacher of justification by faith, but as the great example of how completely the divine life of Christ can take possession of a man and use him for God's glory, she will shine in new light and power, bearing Christ's name before the Gentiles and kings and children of Israel.

Chapter 10

The Heavenly Vision

'At midday, O king, I saw in the way a light from heaven, above the brightness of the sun, shining round about me ... whereupon, I was not disobedient unto the heavenly vision.'
Acts 26:13–19

In thinking of Paul as a pattern we must make a difference between that which was peculiar to him and to God's dealing with him, and those things in which he has been given as a standard to which we may expect to attain a true conformity. His gifts of natural character may be far beyond ours; his divine calling to be the Apostle to the Gentiles, and the teacher of the whole Gentile church for future ages, is something in which we cannot share. The heavenly vision by which he was arrested, the special guidance by visions or revelations which he enjoyed, with the comprehensive influence that he exerted – in all this he is a proof of what God can do to a man, without any ground for the expectation that he will do it to us too. But the more fully we believe this, and give to God all the glory for it, the more careful must we be to believe with our whole heart that the grace which fitted him for his calling will be equally abundant and effective for fitting us for ours, and enable us to be as wholehearted and devoted as he was. Our study of what Paul was must be to us the proof of what God will do to every man who yields himself wholly to his power and to his service.

All this is specially true with regard to the heavenly vision in its suddenness and the revolution it effected. But when we set these aside the spiritual reality of the vision still comes to us with all the force of an example. Paul's life of intense devotion to Jesus Christ owed its strength and permanence to that vision. If we are in very deed to imitate Paul, we need as much as he did, such a spiritual revelation of Christ Jesus as shall master our whole being; and place us on a level with him in his life of faith in the Son of God, and his experience of grace sufficient for every need. Let us just think a moment of what constituted the heavenly vision, and see how its chief elements are to be found in every life.

Christ revealed himself to Paul as him whom God had made Lord and Christ, seated at the right hand of the majesty on high. Paul's exclamation, 'Who art thou, Lord?' is proof that it was in the consciousness of a divine presence that he bowed prostrate in the dust. Christ came as conqueror to take him captive; throughout life the thought that the risen Christ in heaven had mastered him and made him his own, never left him for a moment.

We need nothing less than such a revelation, if Christ is to be all in all in our life. The external circumstances do not constitute the real revelation. Paul writes, 'It pleased God to reveal his Son in me.' That act of divine omnipotence, that entrance of Christ henceforth to dwell in the heart – it was that constituted the real revelation. When the believer is brought to the painful consciousness of the feeble hold that Christ has upon his inmost life, and longs for the transformation into a fellowship, he will learn that he needs nothing so much as just this, that Christ manifests himself as he has promised (John 14:21), and through the mighty power of God comes to abide with him for ever. The prayer in Ephesians chapter 3 instead of being looked upon as a spiritual luxury for the few, will become an absolute necessity for the true life of faith. Paul's example will be the pledge that what God did for him he will do for us.

The second element in the heavenly vision is the call to repentance: 'Saul, Saul, why persecutest thou me?' As on the day of Pentecost the multitude bowed in contrition and repentance before him whom they had crucified, as the first step on the way to receiving the Holy Spirit, so Paul had in the light of the vision to be convicted of his terrible sin against Christ Jesus. The heavenly vision always means the discovery of the terrible curse and power of sin, of the depth of unworthiness, and the utter impotence to do anything to restore what is wrong.

In the life of a believer the longing for the heavenly vision and God's revelation of Christ in the heart, always leads to the discovery of the sinfulness of a life in which Jesus has not had full control, and the unbelief that allowed sin still to reign because it counted it impossible for Christ to keep from sin. The more the hope dawns that God will reveal his Son even to the chief of sinners, the more conscious the soul becomes of its unworthiness, its helplessness, its utter nothingness. In the presence of Christ it dies to the law and to every thought of anything good being found in self. The full vision of Christ and the utter death of self are inseparable.

As we thus study Paul's vision as an example, it becomes easy to mark the further stages of the life in which the vision of Christ is being realised. There is the implicit surrender: 'Lord, what wilt thou have me to do?' It was because the revelation of Christ was in such divine power that the surrender was so complete. God in Christ revealing himself and taking possession of the whole being, is the only true secret of the entire consecration that is so often sought for in vain in our own efforts. Where the Holy Spirit reveals and imparts the living presence a full surrender becomes indispensable and divinely possible.

This again is followed by the open confession of Christ in baptism, a uniting with Christ's disciples, and the conscious filling with the Holy Spirit. Christ had revealed himself personally and most wonderfully to Paul. This did not do away with the need of his being united with Christ's body upon earth. The true vision of Christ will always bind us to his people, and work the conviction that we and they are indispensable to each other, and only in the unity of the body can the healthy action of every part be secured, and the fullness of the Spirit truly enjoyed.

Then follows as the great aim of the vision, the commission for service (Acts 26:18; 9:15–16; 22:14–15). Where Christ who has been exalted to be a prince and a saviour, reveals himself in power, it ever means a call to exhibit that life and to impart it to others. The great blessedness of the heavenly vision is that it enables a man to speak of the heavenly things as one who lives in them, to speak of Christ as one who lives in him. There is nothing that the church of our day needs more than men of whom Christ has revealed himself, and who from experience can bear witness like Paul: it was the good pleasure of God to reveal his Son in me. It is to such a life that Paul continually gives his testimony. It is this that gives Paul's example its inexhaustible attraction and power.

Once again, let us take time to realise all that Christ meant when he gave Paul as a pattern, and let us not rest until Christ has done for us all that he meant to show forth in Paul as within reach.

Chapter 11

Arabia

'When it pleased God to reveal his Son in me, that I might preach him among the heathen; immediately I conferred not with flesh and blood: Neither went I up to Jerusalem to them which were apostles before me; but I went into Arabia.' Galatians 1:16–17

No sooner had Paul received the Holy Spirit but he joined himself with the disciples which were at Damascus, and 'straightway he preached Christ in the synagogues.' The revelation of Christ had taken such possession of him, that he at once bore witness to him as the Christ of God. With the enthusiasm of a living witness he spoke of what he had himself seen and heard from heaven. Though Paul 'increased in strength, and confounded the Jews, proving that this is very Christ,' he soon felt that there were great questions to be settled, in regard to which he himself needed divine teaching and light. He saw the need of revising his knowledge of the Old Testament, with all that it contained of Christ's person and work. He felt deeply the need of such teaching as our Lord had given to his disciples on earth. The believers around him naturally urged him to go up to Jerusalem to learn, in the fellowship of the apostles, what they had learned from Christ. There was much to make the thought attractive. But he at once felt that he might not do it. 'Immediately I conferred not with flesh and blood, neither went I up to Jerusalem to them which were apostles before me; but I went into Arabia.'

The words mark an epoch in Saul's spiritual history. Jesus had said to him, 'for I have appeared unto thee for this purpose, to make thee a minister and a witness both of these things which thou hast seen, and of those things in the which I will appear unto thee.' The Lord had promised him further revelations of himself. If he had 'conferred with flesh and blood,' if he had listened to the voice of human wisdom, either in himself or in those around him, he would have proved himself unworthy of his high calling. The revelation of the divine life in Christ which it pleased God to bestow upon him, was the pledge that God himself would perfect his work. He had been admitted into that new covenant of which it is said, 'they shall not teach everyman saying, Know the Lord: for all shall know me, from the least to the greatest.' He had been admitted into the fellowship with Jesus more close than the Apostles had ever enjoyed; he could count upon it that Christ would make himself known still further, and himself give the teaching that he needed for his work. Though he had sadly misunderstood the Old Testament, it had not escaped his notice that all the great men of God – Abraham and Moses, David and Elijah, and so many others, had been trained in the school of God in the midst of the solitude of the wilderness. There they had found the secret of speaking in his name with authority and in power. God had given him a revelation of himself in Christ more wonderful than had been previously given; and with this a commission larger and more difficult than had ever been entrusted to any servant of God. Not for a moment would he yield to the temptation to seek his teaching from man. Not to Jerusalem and its Apostles, but to Arabia with its solitude, its communion with God himself in Christ the Lord, does he look for the knowledge he needs, and the strengthening and perfecting of the heavenly life that has been bestowed.

'I conferred not with flesh and blood.' In our study of Paul as an example, we must see to it that we do not pass lightly over this, the turning-point in his life. How often a Christian at conversion rests content with the thoughts he had of God in his unconverted state, and thinks chiefly of what is to be learnt of Christ. We forget that Christ became man, that he might bring us to God, the invisible one, might teach us to be at home with him, and enter upon that unbroken fellowship with him as our Father, for which we were created. And we suffer inconceivable loss from resting content with the human teaching from God's Word, while we neglect that divine teaching in which the Holy Spirit from the throne of heaven makes God in Christ a daily reality, an actual presence within us.

When Brother Lawrence, in his desire to live a truly religious life, entered a monastery, he received instructions about the prayers he was to use, and the set times which had to be given to them. He had no sooner begun than he felt that there was a greater need: to know the God to whom he prayed. And from then on he made his one care the practice of the Presence of God, and the habit of doing everything he did from love of him. God became his life, his all in all. There are many who read his life and letters without learning this their chief lesson. It is the same with many readers of St Paul. They know to speak of the doctrines he inculcates, of the mysteries he opens up, of his life of consuming zeal and devotion, and yet have never understood what lies at the root of it all. 'It pleased God to reveal his Son in me.' That was the one side, the divine side. 'Immediately I conferred not with flesh and blood, but went into

Arabia,' that was the other, the human side. No less really than Moses met God in the wilderness, and spent first long years, and then more than once forty days in solitary, silent worship, and so to receive God's law direct from heaven, did Paul receive his Gospel from God in Christ. And as surely as Moses owed the power and authority which he has exercised in the history of the world to this communion with God, has Paul succeeded in guiding the thought of the Christian church, because he, too, conferred not with flesh and blood, but went away into Arabia to meet God. He there learnt the holy art of that dwelling in his presence, of which we shall find such proofs in his epistles.

It was God's good pleasure to reveal his Son in Saul. After that, Paul saw God in Christ, and Christ in God. The vision on the way to Damascus was but a beginning. How little our minds can comprehend the holy depths of that revelation as God was pleased to continue it in the solitude of the desert. The remark has often been made that in Paul the inner life he lived and the doctrines he taught were inseparably one. All that he sought and found in God for his heart and life mastered his intellect too. The inspiration by which the truth of God was revealed to him was no power dealing with the mind alone, but in very deed the life of the Son of God shining into his heart and enabling him in its light to see the truth as it is in Jesus. The experience in Arabia was an educational time in which he learnt the principles on which the Holy Spirit, all his life through, was to teach and guide him.

'Immediately I conferred not with flesh and blood, but went into Arabia.' What a lesson for every minister of the Gospel who longs to be able to say, 'The Gospel which was preached of me is not after man ... but by the revelation of Jesus Christ.' 'It pleased God to reveal his Son in me, that I might preach him among the heathen.'

Chapter 12

Jerusalem

'Then after three years I went up to Jerusalem to see Peter, and abode with him fifteen days. But other of the apostles saw I none, save James, the Lord's brother.' Galatians 1:18–19

Of Paul's first visit to Jerusalem we have two accounts, the one (Acts 9:23–30) is by Luke the historian, giving us all the external details. It tells us how, 'after many days were fulfilled,' in which the time spent in Arabia must be included, Paul increased the more in strength, confounding the Jews in Damascus, and proving that this is the Christ. When the Jews took counsel to kill him, the disciples helped him to escape.

When he was come to Jerusalem, he at once sought to join himself to the disciples, but all were afraid of him, until Barnabas brought him to the Apostles, and told them how boldly he had preached in Damascus. He was with them, going in and coming out, and spoke boldly, disputing against the Grecian Jews. When they sought to kill him, the brethren brought him down to Caesarea, and from thence sent them forth to Tarsus.

The account is a purely personal one, by Paul himself (Gal 2:18–19), and gives none of the above details, but reveals what Paul felt to be the real significance of his stay, and sheds light on its deeper meaning. He had written (Gal 1:16–18) that when God had revealed his Son in him, he conferred not with flesh and blood, neither went up to Jerusalem to those who were apostles before him. He was deeply conscious that God had separated him for himself, and that therefore he was no longer his own, but was to receive from God himself all his instructions.

The attitude of uncompromising separation must be maintained. The visit to Arabia had meant this. He had not dared to place himself under the influence of the Apostles, until he had in fellowship with God learnt the full meaning of the heavenly vision, and had been established in that Gospel which he would have to proclaim.

We now know why Paul waited so long before he met the Apostles at Jerusalem. We naturally ask why the visit, when it was made, should have been so short. From what Luke tells us we might have thought that it was owing to the danger from the Jews. Paul tells us elsewhere (Acts 22:17–21) how, when he had returned to Jerusalem and was praying in the temple, Jesus said to him in a vision, 'Make haste, and get thee quickly out of Jerusalem: for they will not receive thy testimony concerning me.' When Paul urged the plea that his testimony would surely avail because they knew how zealous he had been in persecuting the Christians, he received the answer, 'Depart: for I will send thee far hence unto the Gentiles.' Though this vision has been thought by some to refer to a later period, it appears in every respect to fit in with the details given by Luke. From Christ's words Paul understood that Jerusalem and the Jews with whom he was disputing so boldly were not his appointed sphere.

In Galatians, Paul suggests another and a deeper

reason for the shortness of his visit. It was needful to prove to the Christians, both among the Jews and Gentiles, that his apostleship had come directly from God through Christ Jesus. To the twelve, who had received their commission from our Lord on earth, until the full impression of the promise that they who had been with him in his sufferings, should in the new dispensation sit on twelve thrones, it must have been a great trial of faith to learn that the evangelisation of the world would be taken out of their hands and committed to one who claimed to have received his call from the risen Lord himself. It took the Apostles a long time before they could fully accept the truth of it; it was only after fourteen years (Gal 2:7) that the right relation was understood, and that they openly acknowledged that the Gospel of the uncircumcision had been entrusted to Paul.

In Galatians, Paul calls himself an Apostle, 'not of men, neither by man, but by Jesus Christ, and God the Father.' And of his Gospel he says: 'It is not after man. For I neither received it of man.' Paul needed it for himself, Peter and the Apostles needed it for themselves, and the whole church needed it, that this special ordination, direct from the living Lord in heaven, should be realised and honoured. The church today needs a deeper insight into this truth too, if she is to understand how Paul, without any fellowship of the earthly life of Jesus, or any dependence on the teaching of the twelve, could receive and preach the Gospel in the power of the Spirit from heaven. When this is fully understood men will learn that the great lesson of Paul's example is this, that Christ is able to give each one who is willing to enter into the separation of his heavenly fellowship, the blessed consciousness of having his Gospel not from man but from the Lord himself in heaven.

More than one of Paul's biographers points out how very seldom he alludes to the teachings of Christ, or to the facts of his life on earth. It has been said that the heavenly vision taught Paul only to know Christ in his divine glory. But we must not forget that the risen Lord, who revealed himself to Paul, was also the human Jesus, with all his earthly life taken up into the glory of God. All that Peter had learnt by slow degrees of Christ's character, came to Paul when Jesus himself, as the glorified one, took possession of him. It was not so much what Paul had to learn from Peter, as what Peter had to hear from Paul that made those fifteen days memorable. As Peter listened to what he told of the heavenly vision, and the mystery of the power of God revealing his Son in his heart, of the further revelations in Arabia in which he had received further instruction and preparation for his great calling, and as he became convinced what such an appointment meant in its relation to the twelve, he must have become convinced that the Lord had indeed entrusted the work, which he had thought was to be his own, to another. And he glorified God in him. The fifteen days were to be the proof that Paul had his Gospel not from man.

Let them remind us that, however needful and blessed the fellowship of God's servants is, there is still higher fellowship which is independent of men, which always waits to receive the Gospel from God himself.

Chapter 13

Tarsus

'Then departed Barnabas to Tarsus, for to seek Saul: And when he found him, he brought him unto Antioch.' Acts 11:25,26

In Galatians Paul tells us that after he had been to Jerusalem to see Peter, he came into the regions of Syria and Cicilia, until, fourteen years later, he again visited Jerusalem. Syria had Antioch as its capital, and Cilicia, Tarsus. From the fact that the disciples sent him from Jerusalem to Tarsus, and that eleven years later Barnabas went to seek him there, we are justified in regarding this place as his home during the period. Though he may have at times travelled in the neighbourhood to preach the Gospel, it is evident that he was still waiting for a divine call thrusting him forth to the work to which he had been set apart by the heavenly vision.

The question how these ten years were spent is of great interest. They suggest to us that just as the men of

God of old needed their years of seclusion and preparation for their calling, so Paul too needed his time of special training. The higher the estimate is which we form of the supernatural revelation which was vouchsafed to him, and the divine power by which Christ was formed in him, and made him partaker of his own heavenly life, the more we shall feel the need there was of abundant time for the appropriation, for the actual personal assimilation of what had been bestowed from heaven. The wood of trees of slow growth in colder climates is marked by its superior hardness. However mighty and sudden the power is with which God reveals himself to a man, it never is meant to free him from that law of slow growth which is always the mark of the creature life in the hands of the Creator.

In our blessed Lord himself after he had reached his full stature there were still the ten years, in which he needed to grow and advance in wisdom and stature to the perfect ripening of his whole nature for the work he was to undertake. These ten years at Tarsus, were not all spent in such a life of preaching as we later find in him, but in part in that humble, patient, teachable waiting on God, in which his whole being, mind and spirit, opened up to receive what he needed for the work that was waiting for him.

Paul gives us (2 Cor 12) an instance of what the preparation for his work implied, where he speaks of what had happened fourteen years previously. The fourteen years he refers to will bring us to the closing years of his stay at Tarsus, and we shall find in the experience of which he speaks a lesson that he indispensably needed before he could underake his ministry with all its trials and disappointments.

We know the story well. Among the visions and revelations of the Lord, which were given to him at this time, one of the highest was that he was caught up into Paradise and heard unspeakable words. The vision was so wonderful that there was danger lest 'I should be exalted above measure through the abundance of the revelations.' The Lord, who lived his own life in his servant, knew the danger, and sent a thorn in the flesh, a messenger of satan, to buffet him. Paul did not know what its object was, nor the greatness of the blessing that it could bring. He prayed earnestly, three times over, that it might be taken away. He knew the power of prayer; he had often proved it; but it appeared in this case to be of no avail. All at once he hears the voice of Jesus, 'My grace is sufficient for thee: for my strength is made perfect in weakness.' He understands it. He learns the great lesson that divine power can only be fully known in the midst of utter weakness. The meaning of that unfathomable word, grace, is opened up to himself as the power of Christ's life working in the midst of and through the utter impotence of one who feels that he can do nothing. What he had passed through becomes clear to him, the faithful care of his Lord watching over him lest the temptation to be too exalted should surprise him, sending the messenger of satan to keep him in poverty and weakness, refusing to grant his request lest he might lose the blessing; he saw it all and his heart gave the answer, 'Most gladly therefore will I rather glory in my infirmities, that the power of Christ may rest upon me.' And for the whole of his future life he could now say, 'I take pleasure in infirmities, in reproaches, in necessities, in persecutions, in distresses for Christ's sake; for when I am weak, then am I strong.'

He had learnt what he never understood before. He now was ready for any suffering, however deep the consciousness of utter helplessness accompanying it. He knew that this only was the way to have the power of Christ resting upon him.

Let no one think that Paul ought to have known this long ago. Let no one imagine that even without this, Paul could have been Christ's example to his church for all ages. It is a secret that is only learnt by God's chosen ones. But it is a secret too for all who are willing, like Paul to sacrifice everything, and to wait until Christ reveals himself of a truth as the power of God. It is by those who are content to sink down into the death of Christ, to lie down with him in the impotence of the grave, that the exceeding greatness of God's power can be known.

As we continue our study of Paul, let us remember this lesson, and see if we find any indication of him ever having forgotten it. Twenty years after the lesson had been learnt, we hear him say to the Philippians about his imprisonment and his povery, 'I can do all things through Christ which strengtheneth me.' Let us praise God that Christ not only teaches a lesson, but himself so faithfully and powerfully keeps his disciple, that in all things he becomes more than conqueror. When we strive to form a conception of what Christ was to Paul, and what the chief trials are in which Paul proved his likeness to Christ, let us never forget that here we have the key to all his attainment: 'My strength is made perfect in weakness. Most gladly therefore will I rather glory in my infirmities, that the power of Christ may rest upon me ... for when I am weak, then am I strong.'

Let all preachers and teachers of the Word learn the lesson that lies at the root of all fitnes for God's service. The abiding sense of weakness and dependence, forced upon us by the difficulties of our surroundings and the fears that accompany them, is the true secret of that trust in the sufficiency of grace which assures us that the power of Christ is resting on us.

And let us not forget that it was in the school of prayer that Paul learnt the secret. He writes, 'I besought the Lord thrice.' It is only in the exercise of intense and persevering prayer that Christ can carry on his training and perfect his work. It is there that the voice comes with divine power, and that we are able to understand it, 'My strength is made perfect in weakness.' That voice heard and believed is the secret of a joy and gladness that never fails. 'Most gladly therefore will I rather glory in my infirmities ... Therefore I take pleasure in infirmities ... for Christ's sake: for when I am weak, then am I strong.'

Chapter 14

The First Missionary Journey

'The Holy Ghost said, Separate me Barnabas and Saul for the work whereunto I have called them.' Acts 13:2

When Barnabas and Saul had returned from Jerusalem to Antioch, they again took charge of the church there. After a time, with three other prophets and teachers, they gave themselves up for a time to minister to the Lord in fasting and prayer. Their object doubtless was to know God's will concerning the carrying out of their work. They had understood from Saul what the commission was he had received, and had a time of special waiting upon God as the condition on which his will would be further revealed. The answer came in the voice of the Holy Spirit, 'Separate me Barnabas and Saul for the work whereunto I have called them.' These men had been an inner circle within the church. They now made known to the brethren the revelation they had received, and invited them to join with them in laying hands on the outgoing missionaries, and committing them to the grace of God for the work to which they had been called.

It is in prayer, with ministering to God and waiting on him, in entire consecration to his will, that the leading of the Holy Spirit will still be found, to show us the men whom God chooses to send forth into his harvest. The power of prayer lies at the root of all true mission work. The church still experiences that in earnest, intense prayer, men are 'sent forth by the Holy Ghost.'

The journey, of which we have the record in Acts chapters 13 and 14, must have taken, according to competent authorities, two or three years. Of Cyprus we read they 'had gone through the isle.' Of Antioch it is said, 'The word of the Lord was published throughout all the region,' indicating that not only the Apostles but some of the new converts took a part in the work. At Iconium they 'so spake, that a great multitude both of the Jews and also of the Greeks believed ... Long time therefore abode they speaking boldly in the Lord.' Of Derbe it is said, 'When they had preached the gospel to that city, and had taught many, they returned again to Lystra and to Iconium, and Antioch ... and ordained them elders in every church.' There is no thought of theirs having been a mere passing visit; they established churches and left behind them the proofs of how mighty the work of God had been.

In regard to the preaching, Luke gives us an account of two discourses. In the one we find the Gospel as it was brought to the Jews in Antioch. In the other we see the very different tone that was assumed in dealing with the Gentiles at Lystra.

In the former Paul bases his teaching on the Old Testament and preaches Jesus, as the fulfilment of the promise to the fathers, rejected and crucified by the Jews, but raised up by God as the man through whom is proclaimed the remission of sins. We find the substance of all his later teaching in the words with which he concludes, 'By him all that believe are justified from all things, from which ye could not be justified by the law of Moses.' There is a great contrast between the law and faith in Christ Jesus.

As the result of this teaching many of the Jews and the devout proselytes followed Barnabas and Saul. By the next Sabbath the whole city was gathered together to hear the word of God. The Jews began to contradict and to blaspheme. The Apostles spoke still more boldly. 'It was necessary,' they said, 'that the word of God should first have been spoken to you: but seeing ye put it from you ... lo we turn to the Gentiles.' What the Jews in Jerusalem had done in the death of Stephen, is here confirmed by the Jews in Antioch rejecting Christ and his Gospel. How little one can realise what Saul must have felt as he thought of his own blindness as a persecutor, as he saw how his people whom he so loved were being hardened, and as he felt how solemn the thought was that the Gentiles were indeed becoming heirs to the promises that Israel had rejected.

In the next chapter we have at Lystra Paul's address to the Gentiles, who had come to offer to Barnabas and him the sacrifices due to their gods. He calls them to turn from their vain idol-worship to the living God, who made heaven and earth, whose providence in past generations had watched over all the nations, and who gives witness to himself from heaven in all the blessings he bestows. Paul appeals to their consciousness of a heavenly power and calls upon them to turn to the God whom he preaches.

When Barnabas and Saul reached Antioch they gathered the church together. The church that had sent them forth must know what God had done through them; those who had taken part in the prayer must now share in the joy and thanksgiving. In one simple but significant word they summed up the lesson which God had taught them. They told how God had opened a door of faith unto the Gentiles. It is difficult for us, who have so long been familiar with the thought of a Gentile church, to realise what it must have been to Barnabas and Paul themselves, to see the power of the Spirit of God working mightily among Gentiles who had never known of his law or his promises in the Old Testament. And one can hardly conceive of the joy with which the church of Antioch must have heard of the marvels of divine grace of which these men could tell. This first meeting of returned missionaries, with its report of God's mighty work in the ingathering of the heathen – what a seed it has been of blessing in the stirring up of the interest and the thanksgiving of the church.

The first missionary journey – what an epoch in the history of the church of God. During the two thousand years that intervened between Abraham and Christ there never had been the thought of such a thing. Even the Apostles in Jerusalem appear simply to have looked upon their work as calling for an occasional visit to special centres. Under the leading of the Holy Spirit Paul has opened the way in which thousands have followed ever pressing on to the regions beyond. God grant that the church of our day may understand that all that has been done is but a beginning. If the thousand million of unconverted are to be reached, a great army of messengers is still needed with a devotion nothing less than that of Paul. Let us look up in faith and not forget the chief lesson. That first missionary journey was revealed by God to men giving themselves to special prayer and waiting upon God. It is this that alone can meet the needs of the world.

Chapter 15

Peter at Antioch

'And certain men which came down from Judaea taught the brethren, and said, Except ye be circumcised after the manner of Moses, ye cannot be saved.' Acts 15:1

From Galatians 2:11–21, we learn that Peter had visited Antioch about the same time when these men came from Judaea. Previous to their coming, he did eat with the Gentiles; but when they came he separated himself, fearing to offend the bigoted Jewish party. The rest of the Jews followed him, and even Barnabas was carried away with their dissimulation. While Peter did not agree with them in their insisting on the Gentiles being circumcised, he gave way on what might appear a matter of less importance, and yet was entirely at variance with the spirit and the liberty of the Gospel. He acted as if the legal enactment in regard to the Jews not eating with Gentiles was still in force; as if the Jew had privileges which the Gentiles could not enjoy; as if the Gentiles were not included in that love of the brethren and the full fellowship with them which Christ had enjoined.

Paul felt at once these teachers were not walking according to the truth of the Gospel, and that the principle of salvation by faith alone would suffer, if the law were needed to give the Gentiles privileges which his faith in Christ had not bestowed. Paul said to Peter in presence of all, 'If thou, being a Jew, livest after the manner of Gentiles,' – by faith in Christ – 'why compellest thou the Gentiles to live as do the Jews?' 'We who are Jews by nature, and not sinners of the Gentiles,' – have been saved by faith even as they are – 'Knowing,' – this is the conviction on which we acted – 'that a man is not justified by the works of the law, but by the faith of Jesus Christ, even we,' – the knowledge led to action – 'even we have believed in Jesus Christ, that we,' – here is the experience to which the action led – 'that we might be justified by the faith of Christ, and not by the works of the law: for'; – here is the great truth on which all depends: 'by the works of the law shall no flesh be justified.'

In all Paul's writings one cannot find a fuller expresion of the Gospel of salvation by faith alone than this. The three great words which find their exposition in parts of Galatians and Romans, are here repeated with the urgency of one who feels how much depends upon them.

Justified; man's great need in the sight of God. Jews and Gentiles had alike sought for it in vain. In Christ, God himself has revealed the only, the divine way of righteousness.

Not by the works of the law. This is the religion of man. It was not only the unconverted in the darkness he trusts in; it is the human nature that never can understand how impossible it is. In the churches of Galatia we see how even Gentile Christians naturally turned back to it. In the Christian church, after the first century, we see, on to the time of the Reformation, how universally it prevailed, and how sad its fruits were. Even in the churches of the Reformation, what multitudes there are who clung to it, and even among the most earnest of God's people, the confession comes of the natural tendency of the heart ever to seek something in its own works. This is indeed the religion of man.

Faith in Jesus Christ. This is the religion of God. Jesus Christ made righteousness for us, that we might become the righteousness of God in him. Faith in him, conscious of its own emptiness and impotence and nothingness, yielding itself to the power of the divine Word and the Divine Spirit, to receive in Christ all that he is – such is God's way of salvation. So simple and yet so divine and all-sufficient.

No wonder that when Peter by his conduct gave occasion to the impression that the law could give something which is still lacking in the salvation by faith, no wonder that Paul's soul was stirred to its very depth, and that he did not hesitate to rebuke Peter before them all. By faith alone is his watchword and his Gospel.

After the words of the great confession of his faith, Paul adds, 'But if, while we seek to be justified by Christ, we ourselves also are found sinners, is therefore Christ the minister of sin?' Some of you may think that if we entirely discard the law, faith will lead to sin; grace will be abused and Christ become the minister of sin. 'God forbid,' he cries, 'if I build again the things which I destroyed.' If I seek again the law which I had cast aside in seeking salvation by faith in Christ – 'I make myself a transgressor.' It is not the faith in Christ that will make him a minister of sin, but the very lack of that faith, which still seeks something in the law; that is the reason why any of us who believe can yet be found sinners.

Paul's soul was stirred and this is clearly seen in his teaching that justification by faith brings renewal of all of his life. The faith in Christ not only gave him the righteousness before God that he needed but made him what he equally needed, partaker of a new life in Christ Jesus. It united him to Christ, making him share in all that his death meant as a death to the law, and death to sin, and death to the world. It made him share, too, all that his life meant as a life unto God. In five short, but deeply significant, expressions, he reveals to us the great secret of how the faith in Christ as our righteousness does indeed make us dead to the law, gives us Christ himself to live in us, and makes our faith not only the power of justification, but the power of a life in the Son of God, who loved us and gave himself for us.

Let us note these words, 'I through the law am dead to the law, that I might live unto God.' 'I am crucified with Christ.' 'I live; yet not I.' 'Christ liveth in me.' 'I live by faith of the Son of God.' When we have studied them we shall understand the full force of his concluding words, that it is such a life alone that is kept from making void the grace of God, and lives out to the full the exceeding riches of God's grace. And it is such a life alone that rise to the full consciousness that if righteousness is through the law, even to the slightest extent, then Christ died for no reason. It is the full insight into the meaning of Christ's death, our being dead to the law, our being crucified with Christ, our living no longer, that will enable us to understand what a perfect salvation, what a full and everlasting redemption, the death of Christ has won for us, and makes indeed our very own. And how Christ's atonement for us as our righteousness is accompanied by his life in us as our regeneration, and that these two in full unison with each other do indeed enable us to live unto God.

Chapter 16

Dead to the Law

'I through the law am dead to the law, that I might live unto God.' Galatians 2:19

'That I might live unto God.' Paul uses these words elsewhere of our Lord Jesus. 'In that he died, he died unto sin once: but in that he liveth, he liveth unto God.' Before Christ could live to God in the full meaning of that expression, he needed first to die unto sin. In dying he died to sin in all these respects, the sin that was upon him, the sin that was around him, he died for it by bearing it; he died to it by conquering it. Only then could he live unto God. The entire deliverance from the life he had led on earth gave him access to the new life unto God, and in his glory.

When God revealed his Son in Paul as the crucified and glorified One, he learnt that this death and resurrection of Christ were on our behalf, and that God had so made Christ our representative that we died and were raised in him. And he began to see that just as complete as was Christ's death for sin, was ours too, and that just as sure as Christ's life to God through the death to sin, was our fellowship in his resurrection, and his life unto God. And so Paul here speaks of his power to live to God as being grounded in the death of Christ. 'I am dead to the law, that I might live unto God.' The law as having its sentence executed in the death of Christ, as that to which Christ died and we in him, is now entirely robbed of its claim and power over us. Paul not only thinks of our being justified by faith from all from which the law never could justify us, but of our absolute and entire deliverance from the law, in its claim either for punishment or for the guidance of our life.

In his rebuke to Peter, Paul had vindicated the great truth; by the works of the law shall no flesh be justified. Here he goes further, and shows us that the law which had only multiplied transgression and been impotent to work the righteousness it demanded, had by Christ had its authority over us taken away, so that he himself should take the place the law had taken, and his Spirit should work in our hearts the knowledge and the love and the power of doing God's will, through which we could live a life unto God, well-pleasing to him in all things. Paul had all along thought that there was no possibility of living to God but through the law. But he had learnt that the law, with its demand and its impotence, is the great hindrance that makes the living God an impossibility.

How this could be he has elsewhere illustrated by the illustration of a wife being delivered from the law of the husband by his death, setting her free to become the wife of another. Even so we are become dead to the law through the body of Christ, that we may be joined to another and bring forth fruit to the glory of God. Death to the law in its absolute and intense reality, securing the complete and eternal deliverance from all connection with it, as the one sure and only way to live to God.

'I through the law am dead to the law.' This was the one object for which the law was given – that it might bring us to the end of ourselves, that it might slay us on the cross of Christ, and carry us down into that grave of utter impotence under the power of death, in which the power of God could quicken us to a new life. The one thing that the law was meant to do and that it can do is to execute the sentence of death upon us, that when we are brought to nought, the quickening power of God may raise us to a new life to him and his glory.

'I am dead to the law, that I might live unto God.' Paul is very bold in speaking thus; even Peter could hardly have understood him. In the church of Christ it speedily became manifest how little Paul was understood. And even in the church of today, how few there are who can boldly claim this absolute and entire liberty from the law as the sure secret of living to God in truth. How little one hears in the preaching of the Gospel that joyous tone of conscious deliverance from all that the law means, as the secret of a divine power transferring us from every vestige of legal bondage into the joy of the indwelling Spirit enabling us to fulfil all God's will.

As we go on to study Paul's epistles we shall see how the law is contrasted with, and at the same time annulled by, all the great truths that the Gospel brings us. Not law, but promise; not law, but Christ; not law, but faith; not law, but the Spirit; not law, but liberty. It is as the Christian enters into the full meaning of the salvation that God has provided, and the life that Christ bestows, that he will have the courage to believe that the law with its appeal to self and its efforts, is forever set aside, with its place now taken by the spirit of life in Christ Jesus, the blessed childlike spirit that does God's will because it is written in the heart, and is the natural outcome of the life of Christ dwelling there.

What the church needs, and what every believer who longs to live out the life of the apostle Paul needs, is a spiritual insight into the great truths that our text conveys. No believer can carry out fully living to God until he knows that he is dead to the law, absolutely, completely, dead to it by the body of Christ. To be thus dead to the law means to be dead to self and all its efforts to do God's will, dead to sin and its power to have dominion, dead to every symptom of that bondage which the law ever brings. It means that Christ and his Spirit, God's promise and power, God's grace and the faith that lives in it every moment, are known and enjoyed as the life in which the righteousness of the law finds its fulfilment. It is when the law has finished its work in bringing us to the cross of Christ and its curse, that Christ Jesus takes us up and carries us through his grace into the full power of his resurrection life.

In speaking of Paul's confession of his faith in Christ for justification, we saw how completely the law was set aside; the works of the law had no place or worth in securing acceptance with God; there where we have his confession as to the life in Christ which faith can give, the law is equally shut out. The power of divine grace, the power of the Holy Spirit, so entirely rules in the soul that there is not a thought of the burden which the law brings, of the appeal to self which it ever makes, of the conscious failure which always follows. The new life in Christ Jesus, nothing less than his own resurrection life, enabling us to live unto God, manifested itself to Paul in such divine power that all thought of the constraint and burden of law was forever gone. And as the believer enters into, and abides by faith in Christ, he will be able, too, to understand this wonderful mystery, 'I am dead to the law that I might live unto God.' May God so reveal it to us that the two aspects of the truth may be apprehended and experienced in their divine unity – dead utterly, absolutely, dead to the law in Christ; in Christ, too, truly and surely living to God.

Chapter 17

I am Crucified with Christ

'I am crucified with Christ.' Galatians 2:20

'I through the law am dead,' says Paul, for 'I am crucified with Christ.' When it pleased God to reveal Christ Jesus in him, he saw how it was the crucified one who as the risen Lord had said unto him: 'I am Jesus.' In that vision he learnt to know Christ as the God-Man, who as the head of his body had been on the Cross the representative of all his people. He learnt that in that Christ Jesus he had shared all the power of his death and resurrection. His whole life now consisted in the cultivation of the blessed consciousness: 'I have been crucified with Christ.' There my death to sin and the law is complete; there I receive the spirit and the power to live like Christ.

How many hearts have longed to understand and to

experience fully what Paul meant with these words. And what vain struggles these have often been because we did not know how it is only the power of God by the Holy Spirit which can reveal this mystery. Let us in deep reverence bow before that Spirit to guide our thoughts into some spiritual apprehension of this blessed truth. Let us look at it in its divine reality, in its believing apprehension, in its actual experience.

We start with the divine reality of the believer's union with Christ crucified. We all admit that when God in nature gave a seed the property of containing all the stem and branches and fruit that were to grow from it, it was his power which gave each of them its existence. We understand even so that when God made Adam the father of the human race, each one of his children was contained in him, and shared with him the nature in which he sinned and the death he died. It is not different with Christ Jesus. As the second Adam all his seed was contained in him. When on the cross in the awful three hours of darkness he plunged into the sea of wrath to rescue there all whom the Father had given him, he did indeed carry them in his arms through death and resurrection to be seated with him at the right hand of God. They were there so incorporated into Christ Jesus that each of them was crucified with him, died in his death, and rose in his resurrection. When Paul writes: 'Of God ye are in Christ Jesus'; 'God quickened us together with him and raised us up with him'; he speaks of a spiritual, but most real and actual union.

It is only when we learn to look at what is a fact with God, a divine living reality, that we shall understand how it is possible for us to say, 'I am crucified with Christ.' To reckon ourselves indeed dead unto sin, and alive unto God in Christ Jesus, means nothing less than this, that not only because God sees it and says it, but because what God sees and says, has actually taken place and must be accepted by us as a simple fact. It is our duty to count ourselves as dead with Christ and living in him, too.

Think now of the believing apprehension of this truth. Faith must always be co-extensive with its object, the faith in Christ crucified must take in all that he is, all that he has done for us, all that God has made us in him. This faith is to be like the breath in our body, the divine inspiration by which Jesus Christ maintains his life in us, and by which we confidently rest in the assurance that he keeps our life safe and strong.

In faith there are ever two sides. On the one hand it implies our utter impotence and helplessness, our inability to grasp spiritual truth or spiritual blessing, our absolute dependence for everything on the work of another whom we trust. Then there is the other side, the willingness to yield ourselves fully and unreservedly to him to whom we look for aid. This is one of the deepest lessons in the death of Christ. He went down to the grave in utter weakness, looking to God alone to raise him up: just because he did this he sacrificed all and gave up his life with all it implied to the Father's keeping. 'Christ liveth in me' – to say this means an insight into how he lived and died in the faith of God, and how we in like faith may attain to a fellowship in his life and death, and especially in his crucifixion, which to man is utterly impossible.

Man's faith must always rest on God's fact. What God did in uniting us with Christ in his death and resurrection must, day by day, stand out before us as the divine assurance of what God will every hour work within us by his Holy Spirit, to a faith daily renewed in us by the Spirit. As we look to Christ we shall know the divine secret: 'I am crucified with Christ.'

The truth then becomes one of actual experience. We see this in Paul when he says, 'God forbid that I should glory, save in the cross of our Lord Jesus Christ, by whom the world is crucified unto me, and I unto the world.' We see that his whole relation and conduct towards the world was marked by it. When he writes

'As dying, and behold, we live' (2 Cor 6:9); 'I bear in my body the marks of the Lord Jesus'; 'Death worketh in us, but life in you'; 'Christ was crucified in weakness, but liveth by the power of God, even so we are weak in him, but live through the power of God towards you', he speaks of his sufferings, of distress and persecutions, and of all the burden and care he had for souls as a fellowship with Christ in his weakness and his crucifixion.

Let us beware of seeking for the power of confession, 'I am crucified with Christ,' as a high spiritual attainment, without it being a fellowship with his sufferings and conformity to his death in winning men to God. If we are to say, 'I am crucified with Christ,' it must be proved before God and man by a life in the Spirit and the power of the crucified One.

In Christ the cross was the manifestation of a disposition, 'Let this mind be in you, which was also in Christ Jesus ... who made himself of no reputation, and took upon him the form of a servant ... and humbled himself, and became obedient unto death, even the death of the cross.' It is in this Christ-like disposition that our crucifixion with Christ can be realised as actual experience and power.

We move on to consider, 'in spirit and in power'. There is not only the disposition Christ manifested on the cross but the power he exerted. He overcame the power of the curse of the law. He triumphed over the world and the prince of this world. The cross is the power of God. Let us beware of thinking that our fellowship with the cross is a work that we have to accomplish. 'It is finished!' is the note of triumph with regard to everything that Christ undertook for us. 'Being crucified with Christ,' means the fellowship of the cross, in suffering and weakness, but all the while in the joyous consciousness of an accomplished victory and a complete redemption. Let our experience of the divine reality of being crucified with Christ be in the Spirit of the power of his complete redemption. The cross has conquered. It can conquer in our hearts. It can conquer the men and women to whom we bring it, it will conquer this world and bring every enemy to Christ's feet. Let us learn to say with Paul: 'Christ was crucified in weakness but liveth by the power of God; we are weak in him, but live by the power of God towards you.

Chapter 18

No Longer I

'I live; yet not I, but Christ liveth in me.'
Galatians 2:20

These words tell us how perfect Paul's crucifixion with Christ was. In Christ's death Paul had not only died to the law, and died to sin, but also died to self. In Christ's crucifixion he had been delivered from the power of his own life with its self-assertion. In the power of Christ's resurrection he had been made partaker of a new life; Christ had taken possesion of his whole being to live in him. As long as by faith that crucifixion and the resurrection ruled in him, he could confidently and joyously say, 'I live; yet not I.'

How many who read this are saying: Would God that I too could say it in the full assurance of faith. Let us pray to see what it means, and how it may become ours. It is not the only time that Paul speaks thus. In his grand passage on the ministry of reconciliation (2 Cor 5:14–21), he writes: 'He died for all, that they which live should not henceforth live unto themselves, but unto him.' Living to themselves and living to Christ are incompatible. For a life wholly given to Christ there needs perfect deliverance from the self-life. This is the great blessing secured to us in the death of Christ. He died for all, and all died in him. Where that death in Christ is fully known and accepted, it carries not only the obligation to live for Christ but a real power of deliverance from the desire of the necessity of living to self.

'Yet not I.' See what deep meaning that gives to the death of Christ. In his holy, spotless life he had lived unto God. And yet that was not sufficient. He had to sacrifice that perfect life in death before he could be perfected. He had to show, in laying down his life at the Father's bidding for men, how completely he was ready to give up that love of life which is so natural to every human being, to endure everything of suffering that was implied in its surrender. He gave himself up to the helplessness of death and the grave that he might prove what it meant wholly and only to live through God and to God. He lived not to himself, and that he now liveth, 'by the faith of the Son of God.' He did this as our leader, to open to us the way, and to secure for us the power in which he could do it too.

'Yet not I.' Think of it, how the words are now the embodiment of what Christ's example teaches us, 'Have this mind in you which was also in Christ Jesus.' He emptied himself. He took upon him the form of a servant, or bond-slave. A faithful slave lives every moment for the interest and pleasure of the master. He humbled himself. He became obedient unto death, even the death of the cross. He held nothing back. From his incarnation to his crucifixion the golden thread that ran through all was: He emptied himself. He lived as a slave to God and men; he gave us his life on the cross as a ransom for our souls. 'Have this mind in you, which was also in Christ Jesus.' The chief thought of our life is to be, conformity to Jesus, in living not for ourselves, but for him, even as he lived for God.

'Yet not I.' The more carefully we study the life of Paul, the deeper will be our conviction that these words describe actually the whole spirit of Paul's conduct. In the devotion in which he served Christ and his kingdom, in the sufferings and distresses which he endured, in which he took pleasure and gloried, in the boldness with which he dared to say, even as he had said of Christ, 'He pleased not himself,' so now I please not myself. In the readiness with which he became all things to all men, and yet always sought in all things to please God, he gives us his life-long testimony, 'I live; yet not I, but Christ liveth in me.' And so he teaches us by his example, as by Christ's, that the secret of a life under the immediate and unceasing operation of the blessed Spirit may bear no other motto than this: 'I am dead to the law ... I am crucified with Christ: nevertheless, I live; yet not I, but Christ liveth in me.'

'Yet not I.' Can the believer expect to live a life in which that is perfectly true? If Christ's life is to be regarded as an impossible ideal, this is surely not the case with Paul's example. The grace that enabled him so to speak and so to live is surely for us too. The believer who yields himself to be absolutely possessed by the Holy Spirit, who trusts that blessed Spirit so to maintain the power of Christ's death in him, that all that it has effected shall be his in the same unceasing continuity as that in which our natural life is maintained, may trust that the law of the Spirit of life in Christ Jesus shall set him free from the law of sin and death in his members even as it did Paul. Everything depends on this: 'Crucified with Christ: I live; yet not I.' Oh, that God would reveal to his church what it means to be baptised unto Christ's death, to be dead with him, and to have him live in us that the 'I live; yet not I' may be the spontaneous utterance of a living faith.

'Yet not I.' When Christ died a new death entered into the world with its all-embracing and almighty power. Since Adam there had been death in the world, reigning with its terrible dominion of sin over every child of his. The power of that death, with its curse and utter darkness, held undisputed sway. When Christ entered into death and yielded himself to it, he died a death in which the old death of Adam was swallowed up in victory. His death became a new power in the world; the men, who had hitherto all their life been kept in bondage for fear of death, were now assured that if they would yield themselves to him, his death in its divine sufficiency and deliverance, would free them from the death under which they had hitherto been held in bondage. It would so possess and identify itself with their whole being that as those who had died with Christ, it would be to them too, to the whole extent of what it was to Christ, death to sin, death to the law, death to self and an entrance into the life of victory and holiness. And as the Holy Spirit is day by day yielded to, that death will prove itself to be the abiding deliverance from the life of nature, and an entrance into the life of God.

'Yet not I.' When Paul was struck down on the way to Damascus, and remained three days blind and dumb, without eating or drinking, the sign of the prophet Jonah was fulfilled in him as it was in Christ. In the darkness of that time, he died, as men say, a thousand deaths. But by the grace of God, he died the death of Jesus Christ; he died with Christ and in Christ. And he rose again to find that Christ was now his life, revealed in him by the Father, and that in the power of that life he now could live not for himself, but for him who died and rose again. Paul owed his complete deliverance from the self-life to nothing less than the direct and almighty intervention of God himself. When the believer has learnt the need of this death as the end of living to self, has begun greatly to long for it, has seen how it is prepared for him in Christ, and after having struggled without avail to attain to it, has given himself up to a faith, he will understand that nothing less than the same mighty intervention to which Paul owed it can work it in him.

'Yet not I', will then no longer be a far-off prospect,

but the testimony of what the power of the crucified and living Lord maintains within the soul.

Chapter 19

Christ Liveth in Me

'I live; yet not I, but Christ liveth in me.'
Galatians 2:20

In our Lord's farewell discourse in John 14:17, he began his teaching by pointing out the deep meaning of the little word 'in', both as the expression of his own relation to the Father, and of the disciples to himself. 'Believest thou not,' he said to Philip, 'that I am in the Father, and the Father in me?' 'I speak not of myself: but the Father that dwelleth in me, he doeth the works.' And then a few verses further on he speaks to them of the gift of the Holy Spirit, of whom he says, 'He shall be in you,' and then adds, 'At that day ye shall know that I am in my Father, and ye in me, and I in you.' And, as if to make still more clear the truth that all the life that we receive from him is to be centred and summed up in the thought of nothing less than that he himself lives in us, he says: 'He that hath my commandments, and keepeth them, he it is that loveth me ... and he shall be loved of my Father, and I will love him, and will manifest myself to him.'

As the Holy Spirit teaches us to take in the meaning of these great words, we shall learn that as wonderfully and actually true as it is that the Father lives and speaks and works in the Son, even so wonderfully and spiritually and actually is it true that Christ lives in us. And though at times it appears something utterly beyond our comprehension, the word is sure that this is the great work which the Holy Spirit will work in us, as he reveals and glorifies Christ in us. 'At that day ye shall know that I am in my Father, and ye in me, and I in you.' The deep intimacy of the Father's dwelling in the Son is the promise and the pledge of Christ's living in us.

In the light of this teaching of Christ, we learn to understand more clearly the meaning of Paul's words, 'It pleased God to reveal his Son in me.'

What Christ promised to the disciples about the outcome of all their fellowship with him, crowned with the gift of the Holy Spirit, nothing less than this was what was given to Paul in the vision on the way to Damascus. And from that time God so kept him and perfected his work in him, that through all his lifetime he appeared ready to give his testimony, 'Christ liveth in me.' Without apology, without explanation, without fear of contradiction or misunderstanding, he speaks like a man who to the praise of the grace to which he owed all could boldly say, 'Christ liveth in me.' What multitudes of believers have sighed and longed and struggled to be able to speak thus, and yet have failed. How many have yielded to the thought that such an experience is an impossibility, or have been contented to take their life with all its failures, and consider that as the nearest approach that it is possible for sinful man to attain. Let us see if we cannot find out what the words really meant to Paul, and what enabled him to live them out in their true meaning.

Where two trees grow up in the same spot there will always be the struggle which is to prevail. As long as the

Christ-life has to struggle with the old life or the life of self we never shall be able to say in full confidence, 'Christ liveth in me.' It is only when the life of nature has been condemned and yielded to the death it has deserved, and is kept in the power of Christ's death as a conquered foe, that Christ can truly live and reign in the heart. If we look at the three expressions that Paul has just used, we shall see how his confession, 'Christ liveth in me,' is the outcome of what has preceded. When he said, 'I through the law am dead, that I might live unto God,' he spoke of the deliverance from the bondage of the law with all its appeal to self, its efforts and its works, which he had found in the death of Christ. When he said, 'I am crucified with Christ,' he goes still further and reminds us how as the cross of Christ has been the chief mark of Christ's life as well as his entrance into the new life of resurrection, so he himself had been so truly made partaker of it, that he now lived in the full experience and power of what it had accomplished, and in the abiding consciousness of being in very deed a crucified man, carrying about with him the dying of the Lord Jesus. And when he then adds, 'I live; yet not I,' he wants us to feel that the old life has so truly been brought under the power of the death of Christ that it is no longer he that lives, but Christ that liveth in him. As surely as Christ died to the life that he had lived in the flesh had he too died to the the law and to sin, and to the life under their dominion, that he might live to God, that Christ might live his life in him.

It is plain that it is not until the death to the law, and the crucifixion with Christ, and the life which can say, 'yet not I,' not only as a matter of strong yearning, but of divine bestowal, has been fully realised, and so room made, and a dwelling prepared, where Christ alone can reign, that the joyous confession can be heard: 'Christ liveth in me.' The question will come at once: 'Why are there so few who can say all this?' The answer is simple. The church does not live and has not lived on Paul's level. When it pleased God to reveal his Son in Paul it was with the great object in view of proving to men what God could do, and inviting them to come and see for themselves what the full experience is of what Christ can do for a saved sinner. Paul knew and testified that in him, that is, in his flesh, there is no good thing. But he knew that as God had revealed in him the crucified One as the Lord of glory, so his keeping power could make the presence and the power of Christ on the throne the daily experience of his life. In those three pregnant words, 'Dead to the law'; 'Crucified with Christ'; 'No longer I', you have the deep roots striking down into the grave of Jesus and shooting up into the life 'hid with Christ in God,' with its glad confession, 'Christ liveth in me.'

The thoughts to which Paul has given expression can be summed up in the simple words which form the very heart of our text: 'Not yet I, but Christ.' It is alone the cross that can bring the 'I' to nought. But the cross, in the power of the Holy Spirit can and will do it, and into the empty place the power of Christ's life will stream, and he himself be revealed in the life more abundant that he can give.

The certainty that the full experience is indeed meant for each believer is proved by Paul's prayer for believers in Ephesians 3:14–21. His heart's desire for them is centred on one thing 'That Christ may dwell in your hearts by faith.' Then will they be rooted in love, and comprehend the love that passeth knowledge, and be filled with all the fullness of God. But to attain this is needed an experience not less wonderful than his own. 'It pleased God to reveal his Son in me', that gave him boldness in prayer to ask the Father confidently that he would according to the riches of his glory – that points to a very special exercise of God's glorious power – to strengthen them with might in the inner man. That would infallibly lead to Christ dwelling in the heart by faith.

How little this dwelling of Christ in the heart is known, or preached, or experienced in the church of our day.

Let us praise God that the exceeding abundant grace to which Paul ascribes his life is waiting to work its mighty power in us too. And let us rest short of nothing but the humble, glad confession, 'Christ liveth in me.'

Chapter 20

The Council at Jerusalem

'And certain men which came down from Judaea (to Antioch) taught the brethren, and said, Except ye be circumcised after the manner of Moses, ye cannot be saved.'
Acts 15:1

It is difficult for us to realise what an epoch the Council at Jerusalem was in the history of Christ's church. For this we need a clear insight into the difficulty which gave occasion to the meeting, and into the decision to which it came.

Our text gives us the key to the whole controversy that was raging. Certain men representing the party of the Pharisees among the Jewish Christians, also called the Judaising party, because they taught that the Gentiles could not become Christians without first becoming

Jews, had gone down to Antioch, and had greatly disturbed the Gentile community there by teaching, 'Except ye be circumcised ... ye cannot be saved.'

Let us try to understand on what ground they taught this. Our Lord Jesus had left us teaching which abrogated the law. Peter and all the Apostles acted as if they regarded the law as still binding. The Jews who had believed in Christ and had received the Holy Spirit on the Day of Pentecost, still worshipped in the temple, kept the law of Moses, and in everything maintained their Jewish character. We cannot wonder that men who had always learned to look upon the law as the very embodiment of God's holiness, could not understand how that law could now be dispensed with. In what they had accepted in Christ Jesus they only saw the gift of pardon from the guilt of sin, but the law still remained to them in all its sacredness as the rule of their life. Only those in whom the Spirit had come with power could understand how the law of the Spirit of life could make free from the law with its worldly ordinances. Even the Apostles appeared not fully to have realised how the expulsive power of a new affection would deliver from the forms of the old dispensation. But in those who had not fully yielded themselves to the power of the Spirit, old prejudices and forms gained the upper hand. And so it came to pass that even Christian men could say to the Gentiles, 'Except ye be circumcised ... ye cannot be saved.'

Some of these men had gone to Antioch and unsettled the minds of Christians among the Gentiles. Paul and Barnabas stood up for the truth, the liberty of the Gentiles in Christ to be free from the law of Moses and its requirements. As these new teachers appealed to the Apostles at Jerusalem, and there was no authority to settle the question, it was resolved that Paul and Barnabas with other brethren should go up to Jerusalem to meet the Apostles and elders.

On their way they passed through Phoenicia and Samaria, declaring the conversion of the Gentiles. The tidings caused great joy to the brethren; they themselves were largely Gentiles too.

When they came to Jerusalem they were received by the church and the Apostles and Elders and told the story of all that God had done with them. Certain of the Pharisees who believed raised objections and pleaded with much questioning for the absolute necessity of their being circumcised and bound to keep the law of Moses. A special meeting was convened to consider the matter. After much discussion, Peter rose up to speak. He reminded them how God had chosen him to speak the Word of the Gospel to Cornelius and his friends, and had borne witness by giving from heaven the Holy Spirit, even as he had done at Jerusalem. And he pleaded in strong language that they should not tempt God to put a yoke upon the neck of the disciples, of which he said, 'Neither our Fathers nor we are able to bear.' These words prove what an insight Peter had as to the bondage of the law and the deliverance from it to all who believe, whether Jew or Gentile. His experience with Paul at Antioch had borne fruit, and he did not hesitate to speak in great boldness.

The way was now open, and Barnabas and Paul again spoke about the signs and wonders God had performed through them. Their appeal was just like that of Peter to the great fact of what God had done by the power of the Holy Spirit in giving salvation to all who believe. Under the powerful influence of God's Spirit working through the word of his messengers, the objectors appeared to have been silenced, and possibly convinced too. They could not gainsay the power of the word which had been spoken.

James appears to have been the president of the Council. He was known and honoured for his faithfulness to the law of Moses. In his address he points to the words of the prophet, in which he speaks of all the Gentiles upon whom God's name is called, and gives his judgment 'That we trouble not them, which from among the Gentiles are turned to God.' And he proposes writing a letter to announce their decision.

All agreed to the proposal. They resolved to send two of their best men with Paul and Barnabas as the bearers of a letter. In it they said that they have heard of those who had troubled them with words, subverting their souls, to whom they had given no commandment. They introduced to them Judas and Silas as their messengers of the church, men who would be able to exhort and comfort them.

They would lay no greater burden on them than to remind them of the great danger of what was so common in Gentile religion – the pollutions of idolatry and impurity, and to ask them to avoid offending the Jewish Christians by abstaining from things strangled and from blood. So deep was the sense of the presence of the Holy Spirit in their meeting, making the whole multitude of one accord, that they boldly testified of their decision: 'It seemed good to the Holy Ghost, and to us.'

The letter caused great joy to the brethren at Antioch. To Paul and Barnabas it was a great victory to have the liberty of the Gentile church secured by the mother-church at Jerusalem, and to have the danger of a division between the Apostles of the Gentiles and those to whom Christ had given charge of the church in Jerusalem, averted. It is true that though the Apostles and elders kept the compact faithfully, the believers of the sect of the Pharisees did not long maintain the peace. It has been said that this was owing to its being a compromise and not a final solution. It is difficult to see how Paul could have regarded it as a compromise. What we know of his readiness to become all things to all men, and even to make any sacrifice apart from principle for the maintenance of love and goodwill, makes it clear that he made no surrender to the truth. The same is the case with James and Peter. With their whole heart they accepted what they had heard from Paul previously of his call by Christ himself, what he had told them of all the wonders God had performed, and what they now saw so clearly to be the teaching of God's Word in regard to the

Gentile church.

The Council at Jerusalem gives us cause for thanksgiving to God. The possibility of a terrible schism has been averted. The unity of the church of Christ has been maintained, notwithstanding the great diversity of its Jew and Gentile branches. The great truth has been enunciated. All one in Christ Jesus. Paul has not only begun the work among the Gentiles for which Christ set him apart, but has done a work of equal importance in making clear to the church at Jerusalem what God's purpose is, and gaining their cordial acceptance of its truth. It will not be long before the Judaizing party will prove how little they have entered into the mind of the Spirit; Paul will for years have a sore struggle in maintaining the truth of his Gospel among the Gentile Christians in opposition to the false Gospel, but he had the comfort of knowing that the leaders of the church are all one, and that the same Spirit that was poured out at Jerusalem at Pentecost, will carry on his work to the end of the earth.

Chapter 21

The Second Missionary Journey

'And some days after Paul said unto Barnabas, Let us go again and visit our brethren in every city where we have preached the word of the Lord, and see how they do.'
Acts 15:36

Not long after their return from the Council of Jerusalem Paul proposes to Barnabas that they should set out on another missionary tour to visit and to strengthen the brethren. Barnabas wished to take John Mark with them.Paul had seen his weakness in forsaking them on their former journey (Acts 13:13), and would not consent. The contention became acute, and they separated. We cannot doubt that as men between whom there was a serious difference, and yet how by God's grace loved each other, Paul felt that every member of their company must be a man in whom full confidence could be placed.

Paul chose Silas as his companion, one of the two brethren who had come from Jerusalem. After passsing through the churches of Syria and Cilicia, where Paul had preached before his first missionary journey (Gal 1:21), he reached South Galatia, visiting Derbe and Lystra. At Lystra he found Timothy, his son in the faith, and persuaded him to join their company. For the sake of the Jews he was circumcised. When it was a question of principle, as was the case with Titus (Gal 2:3), he would not listen for a moment to the thought. Here, where Christian expediency dictated it, he availed himself of his liberty in Christ to allow it. The churches were strengthened in the faith and increased in number daily.

Paul appears to have planned to go on to Asia (the province of that name, with Ephesus as his aim), but was forbidden by the Holy Spirit to speak the Word in Asia. They then went through the region of Phrygia and Galatia, and attempted to go into Bithynia, but the Spirit of Jesus suffered them not. The expressions are deeply suggestive. They prove how Paul was left at liberty to consider what would be best, and yet held himself open to the leading of the Spirit to keep him from what might not be God's will. To the Holy Spirit, as the executive power in the kingdom of heaven, the charge of missions had been entrusted (Acts 1:8). Blessed be the church, blessed is the missionary, who counts upon divine guidance.

When they came to Troas on the sea coast, opposite the mainland of Europe, Paul had the vision of the man of Macedonia, beseeching him, 'Come over and help us.' The company at once concluded that God had called them to preach the Gospel there. It was evidently not Paul's own thought to enter Europe; it was God's directing hand guiding him to carry out his plan, 'Who worketh all things after the counsel of his own will.'

The first place where they began work was Philippi. The narrative of what happened there is a summary of what the work in Europe would be. First of all there is the story of Lydia, one that worshipped God, whose heart the Lord opened to listen and believe. Then we have the account of the maid out of whom Paul cast the evil spirit. Her masters dragged Paul and Silas before the magistrate, who ordered them to be beaten with rods and threw them into prison. At midnight, as Paul and Silas were singing praises to God, an earthquake opened the door of the prison. The jailor was about to kill himself when Paul held him back, and he was led to the feet of the Lord Jesus. The Word was in such power that all his household believed and were filled with joy. The next day the magistrates were glad to ask them to leave the town. When they had seen the brethren and exhorted them, they departed. The powerful conversion of Lydia and of the jailor; the experience of Paul and Silas of the persecution that cast them into prison, as well as of the joy that filled them, and the power that delivered them, were a warning of what their further experience in Europe would be. Paul became linked to these first-fruits of Europe by the closest of bonds; the Epistle to the Philippians, written ten years later, proved how the connection had been kept up and how tender and affectionate the interest was with which he regarded them.

The next place of which special mention is made is Thessalonica. In the course of a couple of weeks not a few of the Jews were convinced, with a great multitude of the devout Greeks and of the chief women not a few. The hostile Jews created an uproar. The rulers were troubled to know what to do. When they had taken security from Jason, who had received the Apostles, they were dismissed. The brethren sent Paul and Silas by night to Berea. There, too, many of the Jews believed with not a few of the Greek women of honourable state, and of men also not a few. The Jews from Thessalonica followed Paul and stirred up the multitude against him. The brethren conducted Paul as far as Athens; Silas and Timotheus stayed behind to continue the work.

In Athens Paul found a very different and more

difficult field. There was no danger of persecution; the difficulty was far greater. The Athenians were ready to hear any new thing that might be spoken, and then either to mock, or pass on in utter indifference. Paul preached to the Jews and other devout persons in the synagogue, and in the market place every day. Some of the Epicurean and Stoic philosophers met him and hearing that he set forth strange gods they took hold of him and brought him to the Areopagus. There he spoke words that indicate the divine wisdom with which he knew how to adapt himself to his hearers. Taking as his text an inscription on an altar he had seen, 'To the unknown God', he told them that it was this God he came to preach, the creator of heaven and earth, the invisible Spirit, who dwelleth not in temples made with hands, the great giver of every blessing, calling all to seek him, and commanding men everywhere to repent, because he had ordained a man to judge the world in righteousness, whom he had raised from the dead. Some mocked, others said, 'We will hear thee again.' Some believed, among whom was a man of note, Dionysius the Aeropagite, and a woman named Damaris. Paul appears to have felt that the field was not promising and did not stay long. As then, so now, there is nothing that prevents the Gospel making an abiding impression as the desire always to be on the outlook either to hear or to tell some new thing.

From Athens Paul went to Corinth. There he found Aquila and Priscilla, who had as Jews been banished from Rome. With them he found an abode and supported himself by working at their trade of tent-making. On the Sabbath he spoke in the synagogue. Silas and Timothy joined him soon after from Macedonia, and Paul was contrained more than ever to testify to the Jews that Jesus was Christ. When they blasphemed, he shook out his raiment and said, 'From henceforth I will go unto the Gentiles.' With Justus, a God-fearing man, he found a home where he could receive those who were ready to listen. The ruler of the synagogue and many others believed. Paul must have felt himself surrounded by danger; he speaks (1 Cor 2) of preaching 'in weakness, and in fear, and in much trembling.' In a vision the Lord said to him, 'Be not afraid, but speak ... I am with thee ... for I have much people in this city.' And so he dwelt there a year and six months. When we come to the two Epistles to the Corinthians, we find how large the church was that had been gathered in, what the dangers were to which the Christians were exposed from the terrible corruption of their environment, and with what jealous care Paul watched over them, for their building up in the faith.

Later on when Gallio, the brother of Seneca, was proconsul of Achaia, the Jews brought Paul before him; Gallio refused to entertain a complaint about the religious differences. Paul, after a stay of nearly two years, resolved to return to Antioch by way of Jerusalem. On his way he touched at Ephesus, but when asked to stay longer he promised, if it was God's will, to return again. From Ephesus he went to Caesarea and from there to Jerusalem to salute the church. After this he returned to Antioch. At Corinth Paul wrote his two Epistles to the Thessalonians.

Chapter 22

The Third Missionary Journey

'And after he had spent some time there (at Antioch), he departed and went through the region of Phrygia and Galatia in order, strengthening all the disciples.' Acts 18:23

Each of Paul's three missionary journeys started from Antioch. On the first he founded the Galatian churches; the second was undertaken with the view of revisiting these and then extending the work in Asia. The Holy Spirit prevented this, and led Paul to found the first churches of Europe at Philippi and Thessalonica in Macedonia, and then on to Corinth. Here he stayed nearly two years and then returned to Antioch by way of Jerusalem. The first journey may have taken a year or more; the second more than three years. On his third journey Paul was able to fulfil his desire and complete his work in Asia, giving almost three years to a stay at Ephesus, so that all in Asia heard the Gospel, and the Word of the Lord grew mightily and prevailed.

The fruit of this third journey was not only the direct work that he did in establishing and building up churches, but during it he probably wrote all the four great epistles to which the church of Christ owes so much. The two Epistles to the Corinthians and that to the Galatians show us with what intense affection he cared for the churches he had planted, how deeply he felt the danger of error in life or doctrine, and with what wisdom he guided them. The Epistle to the Romans give us a summary as from the hand of a master of what the Gospel was which he preached.

We have only time to notice the chief points of interest in this third journey. Just before Paul's arrival, Apollos, a Jew from Alexandria, a disciple of John the Baptist, had been there. He had become a powerful preacher of Christ, but still had much to learn. Aquilla and Priscilla, with whom Paul had lived at Corinth, interested themselves in him and from them he learnt the way of God more perfectly. When he left for Corinth the brethren gave him an introduction to the church there. A man mighty in the Scriptures and eloquent, he powerfully confuted the Jews in Corinth. And yet later on, how ever little he may have been the cause of it, the Corinthians formed a party around him, and spoke disparagingly of Paul's rude speech and simple preaching as compared with that of Apollos. This gave occasion to Paul's later warning against that human wisdom which the Corinthians so delighted in; faith must not stand in the wisdom of man, but in the power of God.

When Paul arrived at Ephesus he found there twelve of John's disciples whose knowledge was most defective. They had not yet heard of the Holy Spirit. Paul instructed them, and with laying on of hands they received the Holy Spirit, as the great mark of the New Testament life – a great lessson for the ministry of today, where so many Christians hardly know what the Holy

Spirit means, and need the searching question brought home to them whether they have received the Spirit, and then full instruction as to the indispensable blessing and power of his indwelling.

Paul spent three months teaching in the synagogue. In due time he gathered round him believers who made full confession of Christ, with the result that a breach was caused, and Paul left to find a gathering place for his company in the school of one Tyrannus, a disciple. In this work he continued two years, so that all they which dwelt in Asia heard the Word of the Lord. Paul had not been mistaken in his choicc of Ephesus. As the capital of Asia, it gave the opportunity of continually meeting the visitors who came up to the city from all quarters, and from it there went forth those who could testify of the salvation they had received. At times, in the power of the Holy Spirit, special miracles were wrought. Jewish sorcerers were even confounded by the power of the evil spirits that they had sought to cast out. Many who had practised secret arts brought and burnt their books. And so the Word of the Lord grew mightily and prevailed.

After this Paul planned to go through Macedonia and Achaia, and after a stay at Corinth to go to Jerusalem. After that he hoped also to see Rome. His departure from Ephesus appears to have been hastened by a great uproar that had been caused by the charge that the worship and temple of the great Diana of the Ephesians would be destroyed by the new teaching. Paul left for Troas on his way to Macedonia and to Greece. In 2 Corinthians 2:13 and 7:5, we learn what a burden he felt the state of the church of Corinth to be, and how he had no rest until Titus brought him the glad news of their penitence and their love for him. This gave him liberty to return to Corinth, where he stayed three months. During this time he probably wrote the Epistle to the Romans. From Corinth he returned again to Macedonia.

On the way to Jerusalem (Acts 20:6—21:17), the most interesting incident is the meeting at Miletus with the elders of the church at Ephesus. His address to them gives us a wonderful revelation of what Paul thought of himself as a servant of Christ. He does not hesitate to speak of the three years of his life among them in a way in which very few would dare to follow him. 'Ye know ... after what manner I have been with you at all seasons, Serving the Lord with all humility of mind ... I kept back nothing that was profitable unto you ... I take you to record that I am pure from the blood of all men, For I have not shunned to declare unto you all the counsel of God ... By the space of three years I ceased not to warn everyone night and day with tears ... these hands have ministered unto necessities ... I have shewed you all things, how that so labouring ye ought to support the weak.' Paul could thus speak of himself with all boldness because he knew that it was not he who had done all but the grace of God that was with him. He gives the lesson to all ministers of the Gospel that it is possible in all things to please God, to live in all good conscience. What he was able to say, God's grace will enable us to say, when first we believe in the possibilities of what grace can work, and yield our whole being to the power of that Holy Spirit through whom the exceeding abundance of the grace of God will be proved in us. It was this that enabled him to say: 'None of these things move me, neither count I my life dear unto myself.' It was in this spirit that he could, as he approached Jerusalem, say again (Acts 21:13), 'What mean ye to weep and to break mine heart? for I am ready not to be bound only, but also to die at Jerusalem for the name of the Lord Jesus.' It was because Paul trusted the God whom it had pleased to reveal his son in him, to maintain that life in unbroken continuity day by day, that he could thus testify of what he had been at Ephesus, and what he could be at Jerusalem. If there is anything we need to learn from Paul, it is not so much his teaching, however precious that be, but the secret of his life, as the reproduction of the life of Christ upon earth. Christ dwelt in him.

Chapter 23

Spiritual Gifts

'Now concerning spiritual gifts, brethren, I would not have you ignorant.'
1 Corinthians 12:1

For a right understanding of the place these gifts held in the church, and of the teaching of Paul with regard to them, we must first think of their relation to the whole work of the blessed Spirit as that has been set before us in this epistle. We shall then have the right standpoint for answering more than one important question that may arise.

Paul's first mention of the Holy Spirit is where he speaks of him as a Spirit of power. He had preached to them the Gospel in demonstration of the Spirit and of power. Their conversion had been the proof of the mighty power of God bringing them to the obedience of faith.

The next thought is that he is not only the power but

the wisdom of God. As the Spirit of revelation, he unveils the hidden mystery of the cross and shows forth the deep things of God. And that not only in the Apostle himself, but in all believers who yielded themselves fully to become spiritual men with the power of spiritual discernment.

In chapter 3 he is spoken of as the Spirit of holiness; 'the Spirit of God dwelleth in you ... the temple of God is holy, which temple ye are.' Or, as is put in chapter 6, 'Ye are sanctified, ye are justified in the name of the Lord Jesus, and by the Spirit of our God.' The whole life, both of justification and sanctification, depends upon him and his indwelling.

And then we have him as the Spirit of life. 'He that is joined unto the Lord is one spirit'; 'Your body is the temple of the Holy Ghost which is in you.' The indwelling of the Spirit is the indwelling of Christ in us, making us one Spirit with him. In these four words Paul teaches us how the spiritual life has as its essential and indispensable condition the faith and the full surrender to the mastery of the Holy Spirit.

In chapter 12 Paul's teaching concerning spiritual gifts leads us a step further on. There is a diversity of gifts, and yet the body is one. 'By one Spirit are we all baptized into one body ... and have been all made to drink into one Spirit.' 'Ye are the body of Christ, and members in particular.' In summing up the diversity of gifts, Paul gives a list of some nine workings of the selfsame Spirit. And later on in the chapter he gives another list of eight ministrations with the view of pressing deeply upon them the thought of how the body of Christ needs every member for the full development of its health and the work it has to do in the world.

The great curse of sin is selfishness. Even in the church of Christ it still prevails. Men think of themselves and their own salvation, and rejoice in the gifts they possess. Many enter the church without understanding that as members of a body they are to care for each other, to use all their gifts for the help of those who have less. Their first object is to be the building up of the body of Christ in love. The great mark and happiness of their life is to be a love like that of Christ, who gave himself away for others. Gifts, however truly they may come from God, and however indispensable for the welfare of the church, are nothing without love. It is in the exercise of love that they are to find their true worth and beauty.

In chapter 13 Paul sounds the praises of love. A man may speak with tongues and have the gift of prophecy, and understand all mystery, and have all faith, so that he could remove mountains, and bestow all his goods on the poor, and give his body to be burnt, yet if he have not love, it availeth nothing, he is nothing. Knowledge and gifts tend to puff up; it is only love that seeketh not its own, that never faileth and is the greatest of all. Amid all the contentions and self-exaltation of these carnal Corinthians Paul lifts their thoughts to that one Spirit into which they had been baptised, and that one holy Body of which they are now members, and that divine love in which alone the likeness of God consists. 'Be ye therefore followers of God, as dear children; And walk in love, as Christ also hath loved us.' The spiritual growth of a church depends not only on the preaching, but on the life of fellowship and love, into the healthy exercise of which believers are led.

In chapter 14 Paul descends to particulars, dealing specially with the question of the gift of tongues and of prophecy. The Corinthians had evidently allowed themselves to be drawn away by what appeared miraculous and special. The gift of prophecy, as Paul defines it, 'speaketh edification, and exhortation, and comfort,' was not held in equal honour. Paul says that he would rather speak five words 'with my understanding, that I might teach others also, than ten thousand words in an unknown tongue.' The edification of the church is to be the highest law; those who can speak in tongues are to remember that the speaking in tongues, unless there be an interpreter, does not bring comfort or instruction to others. And in passing he gives us a picture of what a church meeting could be, and doubtless often was, where the spirit of love was allowed to rule. 'If all prophesy, and there come in one that believeth not, or one unlearned, he is convinced of all, he is judged of all: And thus are the secrets of his heart made manifest; and so falling down on his face he will worship God, and report that God is in you of a truth' – a pledge of what can be true of the church in our time, too, where the Spirit of the Lord is allowed free course.

The passage ends with a reminder that as God is not a God of confusion, but of peace, so those who first prophesy are also to learn to be subject one to another. Then he closes with words that have often been terribly abused, and yet have their divine worth in their own place – In all the churches of the saints 'Let all things be done decently and in order.' The chapter on spiritual gifts, on the supremacy of love, on the sacrifice of everything and everyone to the edification of the body, have been of untold value in the church of God, and in the full harmony of the truths they contain, are still essential to the building up of the Body of Christ.

Chapter 24

The Resurrection

'But now is Christ risen from the dead, and become the firstfruits of them that slept.'
1 Corinthians 15:20

There had been among the Corinthians some who doubted the resurrection of Christ. Some thought that the believer's fellowship in Christ's resurrection was all that was needed, and there was no thought of the resurrection of the body. Others, again, were full of questionings as to what and how the resurrection could be. In this wonderful chapter Paul not only answers these questions, but sets before us the resurrection of Christ and of the believer in the full light of God's glory shining upon it, with all the blessing and strength and triumph that it brings into the believer's life. Let us study the steps of his wonderful argument.

1. Vs 1–11. The risen Christ seen and preached by Paul.

He begins by reminding them how he had preached to them from the first the two great truths, that Christ died for our sins according to the Scriptures, and that he had been raised the third day according to the Scriptures. As he had been seen by the other Apostles, so he had appeared to him also. And his ministry had proved the reality of the divine vision and of his call to the apostleship. By the grace of God, though he was the least of the Apostles, he had laboured more abundantly than they all, 'yet not I, but the grace of God which was with me.' He wanted them to understand that his whole ministry and the work he had done among them was the living proof that Christ was indeed risen, and had from heaven proved his mighty power in the establishment of his church.

2. Vs 12–19. The Resurrection and its place in the Christian faith.

To those who said that there was no resurrection of the dead, Paul's argument is: If this be true, then Christ has not been raised, then all our preaching is vain, and your faith also vain. If Christ has not been raised, you are still in your sin. He died for our sin, but was raised again as a proof that he had conquered sin and death, and that God had accepted his sacrifice as our Redeemer. Paul's preaching would all be falsehood; our faith would be vain. Those that are fallen asleep in Christ have perished. If in this life only we have hope in Christ, we are of all men most pitiable. The resurrection is in very deed the foundation of the Christian faith. All his hope and comfort flow from the assurance that he is the risen Lord, our Redeemer.

3. Vs 20–28. The Resurrection, its place in God's purpose.

Christ has indeed been raised from the dead, and that as the first fruits of them that are asleep. Christ the first fruits, then they that are Christ's at his coming. And that will be only a step in the manifestation of the wonderful counsel of God, when Christ has gathered together at his coming all that belong to him. Then comes the end of this present dispensation, and there will be inaugurated a new world of glory, when the last enemy shall have been abolished in death, and he shall deliver up the kingdom to God, even the Father, and the Son himself shall also be subject to him, 'that God may be all in all.' It will then be seen what the glory of the resurrection was meant to be as a step to that final consummation, of which it has not entered into the heart of man to conceive, when Christ shall have accomplished his work, and perfected the church as the body in which he appears before the Father, and himself with his people take a new place in the glory of God, that God may be all in all.

4. Vs 29–34. The resurrection and daily life.

There appears to have been a custom, when a Christian died who had not yet been baptised, to allow one to receive the baptism in his behalf as a token of faith that the dead one would rise again. Paul appeals to this as a proof of how in everything the hope of the resurrection characterised Christianity. And then he appeals to his own life of suffering. 'Why stand we in jeopardy every hour? I protest ... I die daily.' What is it that animates us to such a life of devotion and self-sacrifice if it is not the assurance that this life is but a preparation for a life that cannot die?

5. Vs 35–44. The resurrection and the witness of nature to its truth.

Paul now comes to the question that had been asked, 'How are the dead raised up? and with what body do they come?' His answer is an appeal to nature. Everywhere it gives prophecy of a glorious resurrection. What is the meaning of the seed sown in the earth to which God gives to each seed a body of its own? No one can judge from a seed what the beauty and the fruit can be of the tree. So is the resurrection of the dead. 'It is sown in corruption; it is raised in incorruption ... It is sown a natural body; it is raised a spiritual body.' As surely as the life in the seed dying in the ground is quickened into a form of beauty, utterly different from the corruption to which the seed itself passes over, will the very body that is committed to the grave and its corruption be raised in incorruption. Just as the spirit of life in the seed has the power of producing the plant or tree, so surely he will 'quicken your mortal bodies by his Spirit that dwelleth in you.' Of all the parables that we have in nature of seed sown in death, springing up to life and fruit, the resurrection will be the grandest and most perfect fulfilment.

6. Vs 45–49. The resurrection and our likeness to Christ.

Paul had said (v 22): 'As in Adam all die, even so in Christ shall all be made alive.' He here sums up his argument by reminding us that the second Adam is a life-giving Spirit. 'The first man is of the earth, earthy: the second man is the Lord from heaven.' And as we have borne the image of the earthy, Adam with his body of sin and of death, so shall we also bear the image of the heavenly. The risen body of our blessed Lord now in glory is the pledge and the image of what we shall be.

7. Vs 50–57. The resurrection and its victory over death.

The hour is coming when the trumpet shall sound, and the dead shall be raised incorruptible and we who are then still alive shall be changed. And then, when this corruption shall have put on incorruption, then shall the saying come to pass, 'Death is swallowed up in victory.' 'O death, where is thy sting? O grave, where is thy victory?' Paul no longer argues: he no longer looks at the truth of the resurrection and the glory of the life beyond to which it will lead on. His whole soul is possessed with the consciousness of standing in the midst of death with the victor's shout, and the desire to call upon all around him to share it. 'Thanks be to God, which giveth us the victory through our Lord Jesus Christ.'

8. V. 58. The resurrection and the service of Christ.

'Therefore, my beloved brethren, be ye steadfast, unmoveable, always abounding in the work of the Lord, forasmuch as ye know that your labour is not in vain in the Lord.' Though there was in Corinth much contention and disputing in regard to Paul's teaching, there was a small circle of those who loved him and followed his example, and who sought to abound in the work of the Lord. To such he addressed these closing words, in the faith that the resurrection would bring to them what it was to him, the living presence of the risen Lord. He encourages them to be steadfast, immovable, always abounding in the work of the Lord; they might be sure their labour would not be in vain in the Lord. The resurrection gives us joy and strength for daily service, victory in death, the sure prospect of the coming of our Lord to clothe us with incorruption, all as the beginning of a glory that no thought can conceive, in which God shall be all in all, and we in him.

Chapter 25

Paul's Witness to the Grace of Holiness

'For our rejoicing is this, the testimony of our conscience, that in simplicity and godly sincerity, not with fleshly wisdom, but by the grace of God, we have had our conversation in the world, and more abundantly to you-ward.' 2 Corinthians 1:12

Paul never hesitates in speaking of his being conscious of being holy and sincere in all his conduct. He appeals both to God and men as witnesses not only to his unblameable conduct before men, but also to the uprightness and purity of his motives in the presence of God, who trieth the hearts. He never appears to fear that it may savour of pride or self-exaltation. He feels so deeply that it is all 'by the grace of God' that it would be dishonouring God if he did not testify to what God had wrought in him. The indwelling of Christ was such a reality, he felt such a joyous consciousness that Christ was living his life in him, that it appeared to be nothing more than natural that his whole character and conduct should bear the stamp of Christ Jesus, communicating through the blessed Spirit the different elements of his life of joy and service.

Paul's communion with God seems never to have been interrupted. His faith in God was absolute and unwavering. He enjoyed an unbroken fellowship. To such a man a fall into sin must have appeared to be a terrible calamity – and yet not entirely impossible. It needed a watchfulness that was ever on its guard, a consecration that could say, 'I so run, not as uncertainly; so fight I, not as one that beateth the air'. Above all Paul's faith was a faith that literally every moment depended upon the presence and the power of Christ to strengthen and to keep. 'By the grace of God,' – that included and secured the watchfulness and the consecration and the absolute dependence.

Paul's experience appears to bear no trace of such a fall. Neither in his personal confession, nor in his teaching of others, does one see the slightest sign of any necessity of expecting that sin wilfully committed or allowed, should have power over him. The experience to which he testifies indicates that his faith manifested itself in the joyful confidence that Christ would indeed keep him from all evil and carry on in unceasing continuity the work he had begun.

All this leads us to a question: How is it that Paul never confesses to anything like sins or shortcomings in his ministry, in his disposition, or in his life? He always speaks as if he was living the healthy, normal life, always strong in the Lord and in the power of his might, always led and guided by his Spirit. He never complains of lack of love to Christ or to men, of lack of faith or of patience, of lack of prayer or of zeal. And in addressing Christians he always speaks as if the laws of the spiritual life which he urges upon them, are to be the simple and natural fruit of the grace of God working in them. He never thought it needful to speak of the indwelling sin in the regenerate, with all that our evangelical theology has connected with a daily confession of continual shortcoming. He had such faith in God enabling those who yielded themselves wholly to Christ by faith continually to abide in him, and to experience the leading and the power of the Spirit, that he taught them to expect that God would keep and confirm them to the end. He was sure that God would fulfil his promise to establish them in Christ: 'The Lord is faithful, who shall stablish you, and keep you from evil.' He appeared to consider the expressions, 'Led by the Spirit'; 'Walking in the Spirit'; 'Walking after the Spirit'; such a guarantee for the needful strength for its performance, that he expected that believers could and would indeed walk worthy of the Lord unto all pleasing.

What can be the meaning of all this? Did he really believe that the flesh, of which it ever remains true that there is no good in it, could be so rendered inoperate and so brought into subjection to the power of Christ, as that it never could assert its dominion over the man who truly lived the life of faith? Did he so believe in the omnipotent might of the Holy Spirit strengthening a child of God, that Christ would indeed dwell in his heart as truly as in heaven, and reign and rule there, so that the fellowship, 'Abide in me, and I in you,' could be maintained unbroken? Did he really believe that the promises of the new covenant would be fulfilled, 'I will write my law in their hearts; I will put my fear in their hearts, that they shall not depart from me'; 'I will put my Spirit within you and cause you to walk in my statutes and ye shall keep my judgments and do them,' would literally be fulfilled? Does he not seem in all that he writes about himself in his epistles, to claim that God had wrought this miracle in himself, by the exceeding abundant grace that he bestowed upon him from moment to moment? And does he not, when calling believers without hesitation to love as Christ did, to forgive and to forbear, in all lowliness and meekness to walk worthy of their high calling, does he not give the impression that he believed, and asked them to believe, that by the grace of God they could and would do so?

Or is there some other secret explanation of Paul's motive in thus writing of himself and of believers? Did he perhaps think it wiser not to make mention of his sins and failures? Did he possibly believe in the power of non-self-consciousness, turning away in a moment from the thought of sin, and occupying the heart with the high ideal he ever had before him? Was this the reason of the high tone he took in regard to his readers, in the hope that to set before them a high ideal, even though an impossible one, might influence them more than any teaching as to the evil still in them and the impossibility of expecting that they could really please God in everything every day? Or had he indeed found that the grace of God was so exceeding abundant in him that, year after year, and, day by day, he was kept by an almighty power from the sin into which he otherwise would have fallen? And did this lead him to expect and to claim from them the same faith too? Is this the teaching which comes to us Christians too, through his writings, and can it be true that only because the unbelief of the church very speedily turned from Paul's high standard of faith and holiness to the bondage of a law, we have learned to count it impossible for God to do for us what he did for Paul, and rest content with a Christianity in which the almighty power of God, and the mighty workings of his Spirit are all too little known?

We have asked these questions, to help by their suggestion to a right understanding of our text. 'Our rejoicing is this ... that in simplicity and godly sincerity ... but by the grace of God, we have our conversation in the world, and more abundantly to you-ward.' As we go on in our study of Paul's teaching and example, we may be led to find the right key to what his Christian experience was, and to what the Holy Spirit, through his words, may make possible to us.

Chapter 26

A Minister of the New Covenant

'Our sufficiency is of God, Who also hath made us able ministers of the new testament; not of the letter, but of the spirit.'
2 Corinthians 3:5–6

After having spoken of the power of his ministry (2 Corinthians 2:14–17), Paul asks whether they think that he is again commending himself or seeking epistles of commendation. His answer is, 'Ye are our epistle written in our hearts, known and read of all men.' But more than that – they are not written in his heart alone, but in their hearts God has written what makes them an epistle of Christ, written with the Spirit of the living God; not in tables of stone, but in tables that are hearts of flesh. The law of the old covenant God had written on tables of stone; in the new covenant God has written with the

Spirit in the heart of the believer. It is of this his ministry that he says: 'It is a ministry of the new covenant, a ministry of the Spirit, a ministry of righteousness, a ministry of glory. Let us listen while he seeks to give us an insight into this divine ministry with its power through the Spirit so as to have God's writing in the heart as to ensure a life pleasing to him.

1. A Ministry of the New Covenant (v 6). The words lead us to the remarkable words in which the new covenant is foretold (Jer 31:31–34), 'I will make a new covenant ... Not according to the covenant that I made with their fathers in the day that I took them out of Egypt; which my covenant they brake.' That covenant had not permanence; Israel could not continue in it; it could not ensure their keeping it. In the new covenant God would secure its observance, by so putting his law in their inward parts and writing it in their hearts, that it would be their very nature to delight in and keep that law. As a fruit of this he would be their God in a way he could not be before, taking them up to abide in his fellowship; and they should be his people, a holy people known as his very own; 'For all shall know me, from the least to the greatest,' the least often knowing more than the greatest, as it is written, 'Thou hast hid these things from the wise and prudent, and hast revealed them unto babes.'

All this because of the word with which the covenant closes, 'For I will forgive their iniquity, and I will remember their sin no more.' The forgiveness in the blood of the covenant is so real, and has such divine cleansing and redeeming power, that it brings God's children into the holiest of all, and gives those who believe in it to the full the boldness to expect, as the purchase of that precious blood, the sure and continual enjoyment of the three great covenant promises; the law written in the heart by the Holy Spirit, God revealing himself as our God and sealing to us the consciousness that we are in full truth his people; and all from the least to the greatest knowing him in power. These are the wonderful blessings which the minister of the new covenant is to proclaim and to impart. All Paul's teaching proves how deeply he has entered into the difference between the old and the new covenant, between the law and the letter which could only kill, and the Spirit which could give life in that fullness of the blessing which the new covenant promised.

How little the church has understood the transition into a life in the power of these promises. How little she rejoices in that blessed Mediator of the new covenant, who has undertaken to make them all true to each one who can trust him for it. And how little she has understood her calling to follow Paul in a ministry of which the chief mark is to be that it is to lead on from the forgiveness of sins in the blood of the Lamb, to that written law in the heart in which the Spirit of the Lamb shall be manifested, and the fellowship with God shall continue unbroken.

2. A Ministry of the Spirit (v 8). With Pentecost the Spirit came down from heaven to bear witness that the Mediator of the new covenant had taken his place upon the throne, and would now, as a minister of the sanctuary (Heb 8:2,6), take charge of all who believe in his blood and in the faithfulness of God to make the covenant promises true, and as their High Priest maintain in them in full action the Spirit in the heart through whom the new covenant is carried out. It is this blessed Spirit, the Spirit of God's holines, the Spirit who is God, who gives his sufficiency to the minister of the new covenant, and fits him to testify of God's great redemption and demonstration of the Spirit and in power. And it is this Spirit through whom God writes in the hearts of those who accept the covenant as surely as he wrote of old on the tables of stone. God be praised for such a blessed ministry of the new covenant in the power of the Spirit in preachers and believers.

3. A Ministry of Righteousness (v 9). Paul says, 'If the ministration of condemnation be glory,' – as it was at Sinai, and in God's dealings with his people, 'much more

doth the ministration of righteousness exceed in glory.' The old covenant had nothing but God's condemnation for man's unrighteousness. The new covenant brings us the righteousness of God as it is seen in Christ, as it comes as God's gift of righteousness upon the believer, as it is put on in that new man which after God hath been created in righteousness and holiness of truth, as it is seen as the righteousness of the law, fulfilled in us who walk, not after the flesh, but after the Spirit. The ministration of righteousness doth indeed exceed in glory.

4. And then there is, The Ministration of Glory. The ministration of the Spirit and the ministration of righteousness have a glory that surpasseth all that went before, and if that which passeth away was with glory, much more that which remaineth is in glory. The ministry of the Gospel is a ministration of glory. It tells of the light of the knowledge of the glory of God shining in the heart of his servants, that they again might give the light of the knowledge of the glory of God in the face of Jesus Christ.

And if we would fully know to what glory this ministry leads, we have only to look at the last verse. In contrast with the glory that was seen in Moses with the veil over it, in token of the veil that is still upon the heart of Israel turns to the Lord they will know that the Lord is the Spirit; and where the Spirit of the Lord is there is liberty. 'But we all, with open face, beholding as in a glass the glory of the Lord, are changed into the same image from glory to glory, even as by the Spirit of the Lord. There is indeed a ministration of glory, as the minister of the Spirit leads believers on to gaze upon the glory of the Lord, and they are transformed, day by day, and step by step, into the same image, from glory to glory, even as from the Lord the Spirit. As the glory of Christ in his humbling himself unto the death of the cross is seen and set forth, as the hearts are drawn to believe in the promises of the new covenant, that the Spirit writes in those hearts the very image of Christ Jesus, the secret transformation is carried out, and the glory of the new covenant and its ministry will be known as nothing less than this – God's children reproducing his life upon earth, and proving the truth of what Christ said, 'The glory which thou gavest me, I have given them.'

God restore in power within his church the ministry of the new covenant, the ministry of the Holy Spirit, the ministry of Christ's divine righteousness, as a ministry of the glory that excelleth.

Chapter 27

Ministers of God

'In all things approving ourselves as the ministers of God.' 2 Corinthians 6:4

Paul more than once spoke of himself as a minister of Christ. Here alone he speaks of ministers of God. We shall find that it is by no accident that the name and the place of God have special prominence; it is in perfect keeping with the teaching of the epistle. Everywhere and in everything it will be God.

In the opening paragraph of the epistle, in which he speaks of his sufferings, it is the God and Father of our Lord Jesus Christ whom he blesses, as the God of all comfort, the comfort wherewith we ourselves are comforted of God. In his affliction he had learnt not to trust in himself, but in God which raiseth the dead, who delivereth us out of so great a death, on whom we have set our hope that he will still deliver us. For our glorying is this, the testimony of our conscience that in holiness and sincerity of God, in the grace of God we behaved ourselves. Then towards the end of the first chapter we read, 'As God is true, our word toward you was not yea and nay ... for all the promises of God in him are yea, and in him, Amen, unto the glory of God by us.' Paul wrote the whole chapter under a very deep sense of his dependence on God for everything, and the claim God had upon the faith and surrender of the Corinthian believers.

In the second chapter (14–16) we have the same note, 'Thanks be unto God, which always causeth us to triumph in Christ, and maketh manifest the savour of his knowledge ... We are unto God a sweet savour of Christ in them that are saved, and in them that perish ... But as of sincerity, but as of God, in the sight of God, speak we in Christ.' He not only speaks the Word of God as of sincerity, but as of God, as one who lived and moved in him, and of him ever preached as in the very sight of God. God took such a place in the life of this man that he cannot help, spontaneously and most naturally, connecting everything with him. If we would know Paul's inner life, let us take time to realise what this doxology means: 'Thanks be unto God, which always causeth us to triumph in Christ, and maketh manifest the savour of his knowledge, unto God a sweet savour of Christ ... but as of God, in the sight of God speak we in Christ.' What a glimpse we get into a life in which God is indeed all in all; into a life that invites every minister of God to share in its holy and heavenly atmosphere.

In the third chapter we again find this insistent inscription of all to God; 'Ye are our epistle ... written with the Spirit of the living God ... such trust have we through Christ to God-ward: Not that we are sufficient of ourselves ... but our sufficiency is of God.'

The fourth section is in the same key. 'By manifestation of the truth commending ourselves to every man's conscience in the sight of God ... But we have this treasure in earthen vessels, that the excellency of the power may be of God, and not of us.' Then there follows a recital of his troubles and his bearing about the dying of the Lord Jesus. But he endures all, knowing 'that he which raised up the Lord Jesus shall raise up us also by Jesus, and shall present us with you.' All through there is a deep consciousness that God is watching over him and working in him, with the one object of showing forth his glory and giving his servant the opportunity of proving that the exceeding greatness of the power is of God and not of us. He felt that just as in the life of Christ the presence of God's holiness in him made his sufferings that the divine power might be manifest both in enduring and overcoming them, even so in him, too, the entire devotion to God and the revelation of God leading him in triumph could not be shown forth except in a life proceeding wholly from God and given up wholly to his glory.

In the fifth chapter this dependence on God is brought out still more remarkably. After speaking (1–5) of the hope that the mortal may be swallowed up of life, Paul writes, 'Now he that hath wrought us for the selfsame thing is God,' and then he adds, just as he had done before (1:22), 'hath given unto us the earnest of the Spirit.' He knows that his whole spiritual life is God's workmanship, that God cares for the maintenance of that life in its full strength by the gift of the Spirit, and that it is to this that he owes the power of courageously and without fainting enduring all that comes to him. It is this that makes him say: 'Therefore we are always confident.' 'Knowing therefore the terror of the Lord, we persuade men; but we are made manifest unto God … Whether we are beside ourselves, it is to God … All things are of God, who hath reconciled us to himself and hath given us the ministry of reconciliation; To wit, that God was in Christ reconciling the world unto himself … We are ambassadors, as though God did beseech you by us … For he hath made him to be sin for us, who knew no sin; that we might be made the righteousness of God in him.'

It needs time and thought and prayer for the Holy

Spirit's teaching, to come under the full impression of what these passages together reveal of what God was to Paul. God had so taken possession of him, his life was so lived in God; he was so yielded up to God to work in him all that he would, and he was so conscious that God was present in him, that the expressions he uses are nothing but the natural and spontaneous breaking forth of the divine life that God in Christ lived in him. As one tries to think it all out, one gets a glimpse of how it was possible for Paul to speak so confidently of the sincerity and holiness of God in which he walked, under the consciousness that all that he did was in the sight of God and well-pleasing to him. One can hardly think of a man so God-possessed and God-devoted, so kept by the power of God, as giving way to sin. The Holy Spirit had indeed possession of the temple.

What the power was that this God-consciousness gave him in his ministry, we can see in two of the expressions we have already quoted. In chapter 4:2 he says, 'By the manifestation of the truth commending ourselves to every man's conscience in the sight of God,' and in chapter 5:11, 'Knowing the terror of the Lord, we persuade men; but we are made manifest unto God; and I trust also are made manifest in your consciences.' The overpowering sense of God's presence which he carried with him into his preaching was the power that made itself felt in the consciences of the hearers. When a man not only preaches about God, but gives the conviction to the hearer that he carries God with him, searching the heart, and dealing with the conscience, the Word, is able to exercise its divine power. In 1 Corinthians (14:3–5; 25), he had spoken of prophecy, as a speaking unto edification through the Spirit in such power that one who is an unbeliever is convicted. 'The secrets of his heart made manifest; and so falling down on his face and worship God, and report that God is in you of a truth.' Such preaching brings the conscience into God's presence, makes the soul feel that God himself is speaking; his Word becomes a sharp two-edged sword, stripping and laying bare the thoughts and intents of the heart. Both in times of revival, and in the stated ministry in the power of the Spirit, men have been taken hold of by a power from God, and the fear of God has irresistibly asserted its right over the whole being. A man feels himself standing face to face with God, a guilty sinner at the bar of eternal justice. It is as if the fountains of the great deep have been broken up, a new consciousness of God has unexpectedly reached the conscience, and the soul trembles in his presence. It was this that gave Paul's preaching its power. It is this that makes a man a minister of God, who brings God in the Word into contact with the conscience, and so brings the sinner into God's presence.

It is this sense of God that is needed in our ministry. The expression we use so lightly, 'Ministers of God's Word,' will then be restored to its rightful place. Ministers will then indeed be men of God, 'in everything commending ourselves as ministers of God.' And when the minister gives God his place in his own life, what hope there will be that God will have his place in the life of his people.

Chapter 28

The Ministry of Reconciliation

'All things are of God, who hath reconciled us to himself by Jesus Christ, and hath given unto us the ministry of reconciliation.'
2 Corinthians 5:18

In this wonderful passage, 2 Corinthians 15:14–21, we have as complete a summary as we shall find anywhere of the character and object of Paul's ministry. Let us consider what its motive was, what its power, what its message, and what the spirit in which it was carried out.

Its motive. The love of Christ constraineth us. Christ's love in dying for us had been shed abroad by the Holy Spirit in Paul's heart, and unconsciously he speaks of it simply and naturally as that which moved him, even as it had moved Christ himself. And that not as a mere sentiment, but as a matter of sound and deliberate judgment.

'We thus judge, if one died for all, then were all dead: ... they which live should not henceforth live unto themselves'; the death on the cross of Christ was the complete deliverance from that. And so now they live unto him who for them died and rose again. That infinite love dwelt in him; it had the mastery of his whole being; it was the inspiration and the strength of his life and work.

Its power. A motive may be strong in a man who has not the power to carry out his desire. In vs 16–17, Paul tells us that 'if any man be in Christ, he is a new creature; old things are passed away; behold, all things are become new.' Through his death and resurrection, Christ entered into a new world, and opened up the way for us into it with him. The man who truly lives in that new creation knows that old things are passed away; the mighty power of God in the resurrection life works in him as it did in Christ. It is this that leads him to say, All things are of God, who not only reconciled us to himself through Christ, but also gave to us by the same divine power the ministry of reconciliation.

Its message. 'God was in Christ, reconciling the world unto himself, not imputing their trespasses unto them.' 'He hath made him to be sin for us, who knew no sin; that we might be made the righteousness of God in him.' What a terrible spectacle is suggested here to us. God the Creator, and the world which he made with a view to show forth in it the riches of his glory, at war with each other. Man rebelling against God and seeking to dethrone him. God compelled to threaten man with his judgments and the curse of his law. Man's sin rising to do its utmost in bidding defiance to God's Son, and giving him over to the death of the cross. And just here, where man's sin reaches its terrible climax, there God reveals the greatness of his compassion in giving a Son as sacrifice for our sin. By the blood of the cross on which man slew Christ, God has made a propitiation for our sins, has actually reconciled the world to himself, not imputing their trespasses unto them. In his holiness and love, God caused his judgment to rest upon Christ, and through that destroyed the power of sin. In Jesus Christ crucified the infinite suffering and agony which his struggle with sin and his victory cost him was revealed that men might see what it cost God to reconcile us to himself.

All is summed up in that last unfathomable word, God made him, who knew no sin to be sin on our behalf that we might become the righteousness of God in him. Christ the holy one of God, the Son of his love, was made sin on our behalf, was dealt with as if he had been incarnate sin, was given over into the thick darkness, forsaken of God. He saw and felt nothing but sin around him and on him to the very depth of his being. He was made sin that in the power of his holiness he might conquer and destroy it, and so we might have the assurance of a complete reconciliation between God and us. And so we become the righteousness of God in him, the perfect righteousness of God, as it is in Christ, is offered to us as God's free gift. Everyone who believes in him is united to him and shares his life and all that he has. As incomprehensible as the truth that Christ the holy one was made sin for us is this other truth, that we sinners become the righteousness of God in him. We learn to know it first of all in the justification of faith, while there is not a thought of ourselves being anything but the guiltiest of sinners. We then learn to know it as by the Holy Spirit we put on the new man, which after God has been created in righteousness, the power that dwells in, and characterises the new life within us. And then we learn to know it as the righteousness in which we live and walk, as the righteousness of the law, which is fulfilled in us, who walk not after the law, but after the Spirit.

What a message! God in his holiness coming forth and reconciling us unto himself through the suffering and death on the cross of his beloved Son, made sin for us. Our sin taken up into him and conquered, so that it can now no longer have dominion over us. And we now, just as God met us in Christ, condemning sin, are now in Christ too, in very deed made the righteousness of God.

What a message! What need of a divine power to enable the minister of this reconciliation to speak worthily of it in a spirit and power that will reach the heart.

And now the messenger, and the spirit in which his work is to be done. 'All things are of God,' says Paul, 'Who hath reconciled us to himself by Jesus Christ, and hath given to us the ministry of reconciliation. As divine as the source of the reconciliation is that of the ministry too. The God who sacrificed everything, even to his own Son, to make that reconciliation possible, will see to it that the messenger is worthy of his ministry, and will not withhold from him the needful strength. As deep as was the Father's interest in the work of his Son on the cross, and as mighty as was the power that he exerted there, is even now his interest in every true messenger of the reconciliation, and his readiness to fit him for his work with a divine power. Such a one was Paul, who could say, 'The love of Christ constraineth us' – just think what that means, an ambassador from one kingdom to another, specially in the case of arranging the terms of peace after war – 'as though God did beseech you.' The minister of the reconciliation is supposed to share and feel all the intensity of that love which moved God to reconcile the world to himself, and to act under a sense of the intense reality of how completely and how gloriously the reconciliation has been accomplished. 'As though God did beseech you: we pray you in Christ's stead, be ye reconciled to God.' It is in this spirit, God entreating and Christ beseeching men, that the ministry of reconciliation is to be carried out.

What need there is that ministers of the Gospel should bow low before God and wait on him for that Holy Spirit who can give into their hearts something of the very holiness and love of God that moved him in reconciling the world to himself. What need for a life of close fellowship with Christ if they are on Christ's behalf to beseech men with tears to listen as he calls them to come to the Father. The word of reconciliation, preached by Paul and others in demonstration of the Spirit and of power has proved equal to open the most darkened as well as the proudest heart to the message of God's redeeming love. Do let us believe, 'All things are of God.' He who wrought out that wonderful reconciliation in Christ is ever ready and able to endure his servant with the power from on high that can make his message as a sharp two-edged sword, and bring even his boldest enemies to bow at his feet.

Chapter 29

Perfecting Holiness

'Having therefore these promises, dearly beloved, let us cleanse ourselves ... perfecting holiness in the fear of God.' 2 Corinthians 7:1

'Having these promises' – this is the great incentive, and the all-sufficient power, for the life of perfecting holiness in the fear of God. To know what these promises really mean; to believe in God with the full assurance that he will actually and unceasingly make them true; to yield ourselves unreservedly for God in his mighty power to fulfil them in us – this is what will enable us to cleanse ourselves from all defilement of the flesh and the spirit, 'perfecting holiness in the fear of God.'

And what are these promises? Paul had written, 'Ye are the temple of the living God,' even as God said, 'I will dwell in them, and walk in them; and I will be their God, and they shall be my people.' Paul had in his thoughts two passages. The one (Ex 29:45), 'I will dwell among the children of Israel, and will be their God. And they shall know that I am the Lord their God.' As God dwelt in Israel as the holy one to make the people holy by his presence, so he promises here (2 Cor 6:16) that he will dwell in all those who have believed in Jesus Christ, and will walk in them. 'Ye are the temple of the living God.' The promise secures to us that as truly as God dwelt in the tabernacle of old and sanctified it by his presence, so surely may every believer count upon it that God regards him, and deals with him, and blesses him by making his whole being, soul and body, the place in which he delights to rest and to dwell.

The second text he quotes is from that great chapter in the prophet Jeremiah, Jeremiah 31:1,9,33, in which God declared that he had loved his people with an everlasting love, and gives them the promise of the New Covenant, 'I will put my law in their inward parts, and write it in their hearts.'

Just think a moment what the discovery of such promises must have meant to Paul when he saw their full force. He had gone down to Arabia because he felt the need of studying the Old Testament in the new light of the revelation of the Son of God. It was there that the utter insufficiency of the law of Moses and the Old Covenant dawned upon him. As he read in Jeremiah of the new covenant, 'Not according to the covenant that I made with their fathers ... which my covenant they brake,' – or as we have it in Heb 8:9, 'they continued not in my covenant' – he saw how God himself had declared that the old covenant would be done away with, because it did not give Israel, what was absolutely needed in entering into covenant with God, the power to keep it. In any new covenant the essential element would be the power to remain faithful as the condition of inheriting its blessings. What glory dawned upon him as he saw how the new covenant with the law written in their inward parts, made provision for man's continuing in the covenant. He read (Jer 32:40) that in the everlasting covenant God said, 'I will put my fear in their hearts, that they shall not depart from me.' Or, as it is in the parallel passage (Ezek 36:27) 'I will put my spirit within you, and cause you to walk in my statutes ... and do them.' He saw at once that the difference between the old covenant and the new was nothing less than the difference between the law, with its demands, its impotence, and its condemnation, and the Spirit so breathing the law into the heart that it should be our very nature and joy to do all God's will. He began to understand from his own experience how Christ, revealed in his heart by God, had become the law of his life, living in him and maintaining the life of the Spirit as an unceasing operation of God's mighty power keeping him from departing from God, causing him to walk in his statutes, and fitting him for keeping his judgments and doing all his will.

Paul had learnt in the school of God what the new covenant meant. He had found in it the divine guarantee for that power of the divine life, in which, through Christ and the Holy Spirit, God was his God every moment of the day, and dwelt and walked in him. It was in the faith of this that he called upon those Corinthians, in all their feebleness and ignorance, to listen to the words of the promise of an almighty God, and to believe that there was deliverance from all the sins which now surrounded them. He writes (6:17), 'Wherefore come out from among them, and be ye separate, saith the Lord, and touch not the unclean thing; and I will receive you, And will be a Father unto you, and ye shall be my sons and daughters.' It was in the confidence which such a faith inspired that he said, 'Having therefore these promises, dearly beloved, let us cleanse ourselves from all filthiness of the flesh and spirit, perfecting holiness in the fear of God.'

When Paul spoke to those who were carnal, and unconscious of what it meant to be separate from sin, he pleaded with them, in the name of God's holiness, to remember that they were the temple of God which is holy, and that their very body had the Holy Spirit dwelling in them. In this epistle he again speaks of the temple of God and what is implied in God's dwelling in his people, and his promise that if they will come out and be separate he will receive them, and will be a father to them, and they shall be his sons and daughters. Paul believed in the power of God's Word. He believed that God meant these promises of the new covenant to be literally fulfilled in those who trusted his power to save and to keep from sin. He calls upon them to do their part, to come out and be separate, and touch no unclean thing, to cleanse themselves from all defilement of flesh and spirit, and to aim at a life of holiness such as becomes the temple of God, such as God will work in all those who yield themselves to his call.

If Paul were to come to the church of this day, would he find the Christians so instructed in the promises of the new covenant as to be able to understand his message and to listen to his appeal for perfecting holiness in the fear of the Lord? Would he find them ready to understand what it really means to have accepted and claimed the promise of the law written in the heart and his fear put in their heart, that they shall not depart from him and his Spirit given within them, enabling them by a divine power to keep his judgments and to do them? When the acorn is cast into the ground there is a secret life in it, that bursts out and grows up into a large spreading oak. How did it come to pass? The law was written in the heart of the acorn by God the Creator, and that law passes into every branch and twig as the law of an irresistible and unconquerable life. Would God that his children could learn to believe that nothing less is the meaning of the law written in the heart – a divine power that does not need to transgress, but by the Holy Spirit can keep the covenant, and does not depart from him.

Therefore, beloved, having these promises of the ever blessed and ever faithful God, let us perfect holiness in the fear of the Lord, let us study and pray over, and hold fast these promises as the divine pledge of an actual experience, as the divine seed of an almighty grace, and expect nothing less than that God will dwell in us and walk in us.

Chapter 30

The Grace of Giving

'God is able to make all grace abound toward you; that ye, always having all sufficiency in all things, may abound to every good work.'
2 Corinthians 9:8

Chapters 8 and 9 are entirely devoted to the teaching as to the place that Christian liberality is to have in the Christian life, and the rich blessings connected with it. We shall endeavour just to touch the chief points in the order in which they are found.

Paul begins by telling of what the grace of God had done in the churches of Macedonia. Their 'deep poverty abounded unto the riches of their liberality.' It is still so; very often the poorest are the readiest givers and know more of the joy of giving than those who give without making any real sacrifice.

And what was more, with their gift of money they gave themselves to the Lord. A lesson for every preacher to remember, with the gifts to ask the givers to give themselves.

2 Corinthians 8:6,7,8. This giving is indeed a grace of God in the heart. Paul reminds the Corinthians of the other graces in which some of them abounded, in faith, and utterance, and knowledge, and your love to us. They must see that with all they must abound in this grace also.

2 Corinthians 8:9. Our giving must ever remind us of the grace of our Lord Jesus Christ, that, though he was rich, yet for your sakes he became poor. The Spirit of Christ, the love of Christ, the longing for the likeness of Christ, will cause us to walk in his steps as Paul did, poor and yet making many rich.

2 Corinthians 8:10,11. Giving must be deliberate, laying aside to be ready for every call, so that there must be not only a readiness to will, but also the ability to perform.

2 Corinthians 8:12. Then comes the encouraging thought, a man is acceptable according as he hath, not according as he hath not. Jesus Christ delighted in the offering of the poor widow in her poverty.

2 Corinthians 8:13,15. All must share the burden that there may be equality. 'He that gathered much had nothing over; and he that had gathered little had no lack.' The church in its unity is ever to care that the abundance finds its way to supply the want of the needy.

2 Corinthians 8:20,21. Ministers are to take charge of this grace which is ministered by us to the glory of God.

They are to be specially careful that in giving account they must take thought for things honourable, not only in the sight of God, but in the sight of man.

2 Corinthians 9:1–5. The importance of cultivating the habit of systematic giving, so that Christians may always be ready.

2 Corinthians 9:6. The reaping will be as the sowing, sparing or bountiful as the sowing is. The church needs to be trained to act in this as in God's sight.

2 Corinthians 9:7. Give from the heart and not of

necessity. God loveth a cheerful giver. And here follow the words of our text, of which presently more.

2 Corinthians 9:11–13. The ministration of this service not only fills up the wants of the saints, but also aboundeth through many thanksgivings unto God, seeing they glorify God for your obedience unto the Gospel of Christ and for your liberality unto them and to all.

2 Corinthians 9:14. And even so with supplication on your behalf; they long after you by reason of the exceeding grace of God in you. The collection of gifts not only supplies the immediate need, but it stirs thanksgiving to God for his grace in you, and fervent prayer to him for his blessing on you. Giving has a higher place than we think in the life of the church; it is indispensable as a manifestation of love and self-sacrifice, as the expression of real fellowship, and a calling forth of unceasing praise and prayer to God.

And then follows the wonderful close to these two chapters: 'Thanks be unto God for his unspeakable gift.' As if Paul had said, I have been talking of giving, but, oh, all our giving is as nothing compared with the unspeakable gift. I have been talking of thanksgiving for gifts bestowed by God's children on each other, but, what is that compared with that unceasing and inexpressible thanksgiving that ought to rise from the heart for God's unspeakable gift. Let it be the one aim in all our giving and praising, to be led on to the deeper joy of the unceasing doxology: Thanks, thanks, thanks for evermore to God for his unspeakable gift. That will teach us how to give.

In our survey of all the thoughts that cluster around the Christian grace of giving we have omitted one text, that which we have as the heading of our chapter. Paul had been speaking of the grace of liberality. His heart looks out towards all the Christian life of which this grace is but a small portion, and he bursts forth into praise of what God and his grace can do to supply our need not only in the matter of giving, but in connection with the whole of that life which is simply to be a display of what grace can do. 'God is able to make all grace abound toward you' – note the expression, 'all grace' – grace in all its varied aspects; 'that ye, always having all sufficiency in all things, may abound to every good work.' The grace of God is infinite in its reach, as in its power and its freshness. God's power and his love are united in the one object of making the believer what he should be. Paul had experienced this, that God was indeed able to make all grace abound, and he delighted to teach Christians to believe it, and to expect that the work of grace would be this, that they having always, not a moment excepted, all sufficiency, not a need unsupplied, in everything, whatever it might be – might abound unto every good work. Paul tells us more than once that his life of unceasing labour more than all the Apostles, of conscious well pleasing, was indeed not owing to himself – 'Not I, but the grace of God which was with me,' had been his unbroken experience. He could give this testimony to God's faithfulness, and he longed to lead believers to count upon it as their sure heritage. He knew how slow Christians are in believing in the exceeding abundance of grace which God wants to bestow. He knew what terrible power unbelief has to limit God and not accept his promises in their literal spiritual meaning. And so in this verse – note the five times the word 'all' is used – he tries to meet every possible case of need with the assurance of the omnipotence of God waiting to make his grace abound exceedingly, and to show forth, in every believer who will but yield himself in full trust and surrender, what the exceeding riches of that grace can do.

Mark especially the last words – 'to every good work.' Paul elsewhere taught that we have been 'created in Christ Jesus unto good works, which God hath before prepared that we should walk in them.' That preparing of the good works was not only a thought or a commandment, but an actual putting forth of the divine energy in creating for us a new life in Christ, fitted and prepared by its very nature to walk in good works. And all the cumulative effect of Paul's words here in our text bear upon this one thought, 'that ye may abound to every good work.' The deliverance from sin that there is in Christ is not something negative; it is a divine equipment of all-sufficient grace, enabling us to abound in every good work. God help us to believe the promise, to rejoice in it, to count upon the abounding grace which will enable us to walk worthy of the Lord unto all pleasing, being fruitful in every good work. Let us never venture to think that God is not able to do this until we have to the very utmost made full proof of what he does to fulfil this precious promise.

Let us take home the word with a new and larger faith: 'God is able to make all grace abound toward you, that ye, always ... in all things, may abound to every good work.' What a promise!

Chapter 31

A Man in Christ

'I knew a man in Christ above fourteen years ago.'
2 Corinthians 12:2

We often connect the expression 'in Christ' with some of Paul's later letters. A careful study of the epistles to the Corinthians will show how there it lies at the root of all his teaching. In 1 Corinthians 1:30 we have the great text, 'Of him (God) are ye in Christ Jesus.' Later on we find 'In Christ Jesus I have begotten you through the gospel'; 'My ways which be in Christ'; 'Are not ye my work in the Lord?'; 'The seal of mine apostleship are ye in the Lord.' 'As in Adam all die, even so in Chrit shall all be made alive.' And then in the second epistle, chapter 1, 'He which stablisheth us with you in Christ is God'; and later, 'God, which always causeth us to triumph in Christ'; 'In the sight of God speak we in Christ'; 'If any man be in Christ'; 'I knew a man in Christ.'

To understand the full force of the expression we must turn back to the words of our Lord; we owe to him the deep mystic meaning of the little word 'in'. All his teaching about himself was summed up in the words spoken in the last night, 'Believe me that I am in the Father, and the Father in me' (John 14:10,11). In them we have the highest and the fullest expression of what our faith is to lay hold of and feed on, the highest revelation of what Christ is as man, and what he shows man as destined to be is found in this that as man he says, 'The Father in me and I in him.' That proves what man was created for, what man is capable of, to what Christ can bring a man by his own indwelling through the Spirit. It is the perfect setting forth of the relation of God to man, and of the nature and work of God in man – a God who is to dwell in him as surely as he dwells in heaven. It is in this way that Christ has shown to us what the Father is – God dwelling in him as man. And at the same time what the nature and destiny of man is – 'The Father in me and I in him.'

We do not know whether Paul had ever heard of these words of our Lord. But he had more than the words, he had him who spake the words; he had the life itself. When that life of Christ was revealed in him, it could not but prove itself in that which was its unchangeable characteristic – the Father in me and I in him. Christ was revealed in him as the whole Christ, the perfect revelation of the unseen God, dwelling in a man. What Christ had to teach his disciples in words he communicated to Paul as a living reality. Christ revealed in the heart of Paul meant above all, God revealed in Christ. This explains that intense consciousness of the inseparable union between the Father and the Son which we find in all the salutations, and throughout all the epistles. This leads us on to the full meaning of Paul's gospel, Christ dwelling in the heart by faith, and so the man filled with all the fullness of God.

When Christ had thus revealed the secret of the Father being in him and he in the Father, he went on, in connection with the promise of the Holy Spirit, to speak of the union between himself and his disciples as equally intimate, 'In that day ye shall know that ye are in me, and I in you.' That little word 'in' with its revelation of the mystery of the father in the Son, becomes the signature of the relationship between the Son and his redeemed disciple. Our Lord then goes on to give us the picture in his mind of what the true disciple is. Five times he repeats the word, 'If a man love me, he will keep my commandments.' 'If ye keep my commandments ye shall abide in my love.' 'Ye are my friends, if ye do the things which I command you.' This picture in the mind of Christ is held up for our faith to lay hold of and to claim. It is the pledge of what Christ in his redemption has made possible, has made positively certain for us. As long as the words are to us like a command of Moses, an impossible ideal, we shrink back from it as something beyond our reach. But when we understand what it means to be saved by faith, by the faith that not only claims Christ's revelation of himself, the Father in me, and I in him, but equally the revelation of the disciple as Christ abides in him and he in Christ, loving him and keeping his commandments, we shall take courage for the assurance that our surrender to live it out will be accepted and honoured.

The teaching of Christ in the last night had reference to the new dispensation in the power of the endless life, in the power of the Holy Spirit, which was to follow upon his ascension. All Paul's teaching was to be the exposition and enforcement of it. In his own life he was to prove how wonderfully Christ filled out the picture he had drawn. As intense and all-controlling as was Paul's faith in the Christ who said, 'The Father in me and I in him,' was his faith too in the disciple of whom Christ spoke, 'Abide in me and I in you.' 'If a man love me, he will keep my words ... and we will come and make our abode with him.'

Do these thoughts not suggest what Paul meant by the use of the expression in his teaching, 'Ye are in Christ' and when he says of himself, 'A man in Christ.' It bids us remember that there are two aspects, the one that wonderful, omnipotent grace of God by which we are God's workmanship, created in Christ Jesus, so that if any man is in Christ he is a new creature. God has planted him in Christ. God establishes him in Christ; it is of God that he is in Christ Jesus, Who is made of God everything to us that we can need. And then on the other hand it calls us to the exercise of an unceasing faith that the Christ in whom we are will be to us the Christ in us. That faith makes us strong to keep his commandments and to abide in his love. That faith wakens in us an entirely new consciousness of our position before God and the world. It enables us to live in the words of Christ. 'Ye in me, and I in you,' as actual realities, as the sure and certain hope of what he will carry out in us. It will lead us on until the thought of our place as a man in Christ gets dominion over our whole being, and becomes the secret consciousness of all our walk before God and before the world.

'A man in Christ.' What a study for our faith to appropriate fully. What a call to worship and adore as we think of the eternal God having planted us into Christ, and of the living ever keeping watch over us and maintaining the unbroken communion with each one who will yield himself to trust his mighty grace. 'I knew a man in Christ above fourteen years ago.' May each of us live in the consciousness of what it means: 'A man in Christ.'

Chapter 32

The Cross and the Spirit

'O foolish Galatians, before whose eyes Jesus Christ was openly set forth crucified, … received ye the Spirit by the works of the law, or by the hearing of faith?' Galatians 3:1,2

It is often said that justification by faith is the central truth of this epistle. The statement is hardly correct. There are two passages dealing specially with this truth – chapter 2:16 and chapter 3:6–14. It is but a portion of the larger truth that the epistle deals with – the true Christian life as it has its beginnings in justification, its growth and strength in the power of Christ's cross and Spirit. I do not think that a better summary can be given of the doctrinal and practical teaching in the four last chapters than in the words – The cross and the Spirit.

Note how in our text they form the starting point of

the appeal, and how intimately they are connected. I preached Christ crucified to you; you received the Holy Spirit through that preaching. It came not by the works of the law, but by the hearing of faith. From that he passes on (3:6–12) to Abraham, with the promise that God would justify the Gentiles by faith. So far was the law from justifying that it could do nothing but bring a curse (vs 10–12). Christ redeemed us from the curse, having become a curse for us on the cross, 'that the blessing of Abraham might come on the Gentiles through Jesus Christ; that we might receive the promise of the Spirit through faith.' Note carefully how here (v 14) as in the opening verses, the great work of the cross is that through it we receive the Spirit. The law is not only impotent to justify, and is therefore set aside by the Cross, which delivers us from the curse, but the law is equally impotent, when we have been redeemed to guide us in God's service. As a rule of life it is set aside by the power of the Holy Spirit, teaching us to know and to do the will of God. The Jews thought the law could justify, and the law could enable a man to maintain the life of justification before God. The Gospel comes to free us utterly and forever from the law. The Cross takes away the curse of sin; crucified with Christ we are dead to the law. The Spirit keeps us from the power of sin as it dwells in the flesh; it does what the law never could do. It teaches us with the heart to know and to love and to do the will of God. The Cross and the Spirit are the two great powers of the Christian life, never to be separated. It is only the two together that can give us complete and permanent deliverance from the power of the flesh, which ever seeks to bring us again in bondage to the law.

In the second half of the chapter (3:15–29), Paul answers the question, What then is the law, and for what purpose did God give it? He reminds us that the promises and the covenant to Abraham had been given 400 years before the law; that it was added, long after the promise (because of transgression) that by the law the knowledge of sin might come, and man learn his own sinfulness, and be brought to feel his need of a Saviour. He speaks of the law as the keeper of a prison in which we as criminals are shut up under sin 'until the seed should come,' and faith be revealed; as a tutor, or schoolmaster to bring us to Christ; as a guardian or steward under which we are held in bondage, until the fullness of time came. Now that Christ has come, now that faith has come, now that the Spirit has come, now we are no longer like bondservants, but truly sons of God through Jesus Christ.

Mark how at the close of this exposition of what the law means, and what alone it can do, to prepare the way for Christ, Paul in chapter 4:4–7 again points out the vital and essential connection between the cross and the Spirit. 'God sent forth his Son ... to redeem them that were under the law, that we might receive the adoption of sons.' And then, 'Because ye are sons, God hath sent forth the Spirit of his Son into your hearts ... Wherefore thou art no more a servant," – ruled by the law – "but a son; and if a son, then an heir of God through Christ.' It was under the sense of how much they needed the full experience of the power of Christ's redemption on the Cross and his Spirit in the heart, that he writes, 'I travail in birth again until Christ be formed in you.' and it is with this view, too, that he ends the chapter with the allegory of Ishamael and Isaac. The one child born in bondage, the type of men under the law; the other, born of Jerusalem, which is above and is free, the heir according to the covenant, free from the law and the flesh and the world.

Paul had been admired for the power with which he met every argument and prejudice of the Jews, and proved from the Old Testament itself that the law was meant to give place to new dispensation of infinitely greater glory. There is one aspect of Paul's teaching that has not been properly emphasised. It is this, that the truths he unfolds are just what the church of today, after 1900 years, is in need of. Through the illumination of the divine Spirit he saw that the question of legalism was not only a thing to which the Christian Jews were clinging. It was something hidden in the natural heart that led men always to seek for external commands and observances, by which they might regulate their conduct and secure God's favour. The law appeals to a man's power, encourages his efforts, rouses his will, excites his hope, and then fosters his pride. The law appeals to self and to the flesh, and leads to a religion in which the mind of the flesh and the will of the flesh have free scope. It is not only with those who reject God's Word, but with multitudes of Christians, that the effort to obey God's will either leads to self-contentment or ends in utter despair of success.

This epistle brings to the church of today just what it needs. Would God that ministers of the Gospel knew to bring it home to needy hearts. It tells us of Christ crucified as at once the object of the preaching of faith, and the way to receive the Spirit. It tells of the law, that can indeed do nothing but bring down a curse, and of the cross that bore that curse and took it for ever away. It tells of faith in Christ and his cross as the immediate and sufficient deliverance for every troubled soul. It tells of the Spirit that is received to dwell in the heart, the Spirit of childlike liberty, the Spirit of life and love and power breathing within us. This Spirit is the very principle in our inmost being of all the graces that can please God and bless men and keep our hearts in never-ceasing peace. It invites us through faith to union and identification with Christ, which will enable us boldly to say, 'I am crucified with Christ ... Christ liveth in me.' And it promises us that what God did for Paul shall be done in us, revealing his Son in us, and what Paul yearned for in the Galatians, that Christ might be formed in them, may, in very deed, become our portion. All and only and most surely through the cross and the Spirit of Jesus.

Chapter 33

Contrasts to the Law

'That no man is justified by the law in the sight of God, it is evident: for, The just shall live by faith. And the law is not of faith: but, The man that doeth them shall live in them.'
Galatians 3:11–12

To understand fully the argument of the epistle to the Galatians, and to enter by experience into the blessed life of liberty that it offers us, we need to get a true insight into what the law means. There is on the one hand the utter hopelessness of obtaining God's favour through it, and on the other the complete deliverance from it that there is in Christ Jesus. The study of the various contrasts to the law which the epistle gives us will help us to a deeper insight into the salvation which Christ has brought us.

The first contrast is: The Law and Faith. The words of our text make this very clear by the two quotations from the Word of God. The one tells us 'the just shall live by faith.' The other speaks of the works of the law, 'the man that doeth them shall live in them.' Both passages speak of life, but there is an infinite difference in the path of life which they hold out. The one says, Believe and live. The other says, Do and live. The one teaches to believe in God and what he does for us. The other to do our utmost to obey God and his commandments. The latter, the way of life through the law, is the path that human nature counts the true one, because it knows not the holiness of God, and the utter impossibility of our really fulfilling the law. It is blind to its deep corruption and impotence, and satisfies itself with such an external observance of the commandments as can satisfy men. It has never learnt that God gave it as a training school to teach men their sinfulness, to draw them to seek for his mercy and to lead them on to Christ. It has never understood that the law contained within itself the germ of its own insufficiency, in the words, 'Cursed is everyone that continueth not in all things that are written in the book of the law to do them.'

To those who have understood the purpose of the law, and yielded themselves to it first as it arouses the desire after God and his righteousness and then to the sense of their own sinfulness and helplessness, the other word comes, as one of infinite hope and blessedness: 'The just shall live by faith.' Come to God with your sin and the prayer, 'God be merciful to me a sinner,' come in the faith of his grace, of his promise, of his Son, of his Spirit, and all that they have engaged to work for you and in you with divine power, and you shall live. This is God's way to life and to glory. The gospel is simply God's message pleading with us to have done with the law and through faith to find our life in himself. The law and faith – blessed is the man who has entered fully and with his whole heart into the meaning of the contrast.

The Law and Grace. Paul had said to Peter (Galatians 2:21) 'I do not frustrate the grace of God: for if righteousness come by the law, then Christ is dead in vain,' there is no place for grace. And in chapter 5 he says again (v 4), 'Whosoever of you are justified by the law; ye are fallen from grace.' Grace is the infinite mercy that receives and blesses the sinner without the thought of merit. Grace is also the infinite power that works in him all that God commands. Law and grace are at deadly variance, and the great reason that grace cannot do its perfect work is that there still clings to us the secret desire, at least to some small extent, to fulfil the law's demands. Strange – one would think that man would accept with joy and gratitude God's offer to work in him everything that is pleasing in his sight. And yet the heart is ever ready to trust to its own efforts for what God has offered as a free gift.

Law and Promise. Faith always must have a promise to rest upon. It was God's promise to Abraham that made him strong in faith. Paul teaches us that that promise was given four hundred years before the law. The law came by way of parenthesis to prepare for the complete fulfilment of the promise. The promise gives; the law demands. The promise, in its limitless reach, holds out the prospect of what God, with all the riches of his glory, will do for us. What folly to neglect the promise and its offer of the glorious liberty of the children of God, and abide in the bondage of the law. What perfect blessedness when the sinner begins to know the God who has given the promise and will fulfil it, and learns by faith alone to live on it.

Law and Christ. The sum and centre of all God's promises in Jesus Christ. In the first promise in Paradise, in the promise of blessing to Abraham, in all God's dealings with mankind, Jesus Christ is all in all. He came to fulfil the law for us. He came to bear the curse for us. He came to bring the divine life down into human nature. He came in dying to give himself for us and impart the very life he himself had lived. He came to destroy death and to rise to the throne of God, that thence he might give his own Spirit to dwell in our hearts, and make himself ever-present there. He came to be himself the living law of life dwelling in the heart by the Spirit bringing forth fruit unto God. We need not wonder that Paul wrote, 'O foolish Galatians, who hath bewitched you?' But how much more have we reason to wonder that Christians who profess to know and love the Bible, to know and love the Lord Jesus, should still so continually yield to the legal spirit, and refuse that implicit and abiding faith in Jesus of which he is so worthy, and in which alone the abounding life is to be found.

The Law and God. What a contrast! The law which God gave to bring man to himself became, through man's blindness and pride, the veil that hid God from him. The law which was to bring man to seek the righteousness that God alone could bestow, and so bring him into fellowship with himself, became the pedestal on which he exalted himself against God. What a mystery of grace that God should have given his own Son, that in him the fierce judgment of the law might be executed, and a divine deliverance effected by which men might become the sons of God. With the very Spirit and likeness of his Son in their hearts, they fulfil all the righteousness of the law, as those who live not after the flesh but after the Spirit. What a Gospel! To come out from the law and its bondage to God and his love.

The Law and the Spirit. 'If ye be led by the Spirit, ye are not under the law.' God's promise to Abraham aimed at this. Christ's bearing the cross secured this. The preaching of the Gospel among the Galatians effected this. This was the Gospel that Paul preached in this epistle. Christ and his righteousness, justification by faith and its blessings avail little, they are beyond our reach, except as the Spirit dwells in us and makes Christ and all there is in him a living reality within us. The great defect of the law was that it could not give life (Galatians 3:21). It was something external, it could not change the heart. The Spirit came to give the new heart, and himself, so to become the law of our inmost nature that the affection and the will should delight, even as Christ, in nothing but doing the will of the Father. Praise God, for the complete salvation, the Spirit of his Son given into our hearts.

The Law and the Cross. The law brings man nothing but a curse. It spoke, 'Cursed is every one that continueth not to do them.' And again, 'Cursed is every one that hangeth on a tree.' The cross reveals that double curse in Christ, who became a curse for us, and redeemed us from the curse. And so the cross became the source and the symbol of blessing, and of life eternal. In it and its atonement we find Christ our righteousness; Christ satisfies all the demands of the law. In it and its fellowship we find our life. The disposition that accepted and approved of the sentence of death, the obedience that yielded itself to God's will, the love that gave up its life for men, as we gaze upon the cross and claim its power, becomes ours. At first the cross looks a more terrible burden than even the law. But as we believe in it and yield to it, it becomes to us the power of God, and we can say, 'I bear it, and am borne by it. I hold it, and am held.' Oh, listen, all who are seeking for peace and holiness, the voice cries, 'Come away from the law, let Christ and his cross be your home and your joy, and let your watchword be, 'Not the law and the death it brings, but the cross, and the life it bestows.'

One more thought. How wonderfully all these contrasts are gathered up in the one word, 'Only believe'. As faith feeds upon the promise, yields itself to grace, lives and abides in Christ, receives and counts upon God the Spirit to reveal and to impart the presence of God himself, we begin to know aright what it is to be saved by faith, to live by faith, believing to rejoice with joy unspeakable and full of glory.

May God reveal to us every vestige of the legal spirit that there is still in us, and strengthen in us the faith that what the law could not do, God can and will do, 'exceeding abundantly above all that we can ask or think.'

Chapter 34

The Spirit of God's Son

'God sent forth his Son ... to redeem them that were under the law, that we might receive the adoption of sons. And because ye are sons, God hath sent forth the Spirit of his Son into your hearts, crying, Abba, Father.' Galatians 4:4–6

In studying the contrast between the law and the Spirit, we were reminded of the claim the law had upon a man's whole life and being. The law of God was meant to cover everything, searching down even into the depths of the heart. And equally so the law in its human aspect, as the self-righteous Pharisee strove to keep it, entered into the minutest details of his daily life. If the Spirit was really to accomplish for us what the law could not do, he must have the power of mastering our whole inward and outward nature, and enabling us in everything to be well-pleasing to God. What the law could not do in that it was weak through the flesh, in that it could give no life, the Spirit of Christ could in very deed effect for us; he could work within us in God's almighty power all God's will, he could, in the deepest meaning of the word, give us a new life, the very life of God himself.

Until the Christian grasps this, the Holy Spirit cannot exert his full power in him. In giving us the Spirit God assures us that our own impotence need be no hindrance in the way of carrying out his will. The Spirit is given us with the express purpose and promise that the life of a child of God is actually possible because he has become the law of our being, its inmost nature, its all-sufficient strength, its divine life. God never asks us that we should in our own strength fulfil his command. In calling us to be children he bestowed upon us this wonderful gift, the Spirit of his Son; the Spirit by whom Christ was led all his life, through whom he offered himself without spot a sacrifice unto God. This very same Spirit will, if we yield to him and wait upon him, work in us even as he did in Christ, and transform us into his likeness.

God sent forth the Spirit of his Son. The words suggest to us the thought of the intimate relation between Christ and the Spirit, and what that relationship implies. God sent forth the Spirit of his Son; the mission of the Spirit has the same divine source and authority as the mission of the Son. As the Son whom the Father sent forth was God, even so the Spirit. As we justly insist upon the faith in the divine nature of the Son as essential to our experience of his full redemption, even so with the blessed Spirit. To know that he is God, that God himself through him works out in us the salvation that has been prepared in Christ, to yield ourselves with that entire surrender that he claims as God, is a thought to which many believers are strange, and without which the experience of the divine life must needs be deeply defective.

The Spirit is the Spirit of the Son. One of the great objects of Christ's living a human life in this world was to show us what the life of man ought to be, a life in the flesh wholly given up and yielded to God's disposal. When Christ died it was that he might impart his own life to all who believe in him. When God sent the Spirit of that Son whom he had sent forth, it was as the pledge and the power of receiving and living out that life of Christ. As Paul puts it in this epistle, Christ redeemed us from the curse that we might receive the promise of the Spirit by faith. Christ redeemed us who were under the law that as children of God we might have the very same Spirit that the Son had sent into our heart crying 'Abba Father'. The teaching concerning the Holy Spirit in this epistle is not meant to be, as many believe, simply the application of the great truth of our redemption by Christ and our justification by faith. It is far more, its object is to show us the intense and perfect unity of the two parts of our redemption – God sending his Son to redeem us to the adoption of sons; God sending the Spirit of his Son, enabling us to live in human flesh the life of a heaven-born child of the Father.

No wonder that the church which separates what God has joined together and counts the truth about the Son and his divinity as of more importance than of the Holy Spirit and his mission, cannot walk in that divine power of the Holy Spirit for which we have been redeemed by Christ. As supernatural, as essential as is the mission of the Son, is the mission of the Spirit too.

It has been said that the great work of the Spirit is, not to create a Spirit-consciousness, but a Christ-consciousness. Most true – and yet it is but half a truth. The only true and full Christ-consciousness is that which bears the stamp and mark of the Spirit upon it. It is very possible to find the Christ-consciousness strong in a writer, or a preacher, or a Christian, without any mark of its being the Spirit – wrought consciousness which comes from above. Education, and study and zeal for evangelical truth may make a man willing to stand up boldly for all that Scripture reveals of Christ, and to be ready to give his life for it, while yet the demonstration of the Spirit and of power may be sadly lacking. The great need of the church and the believer is to know that just as the Father and the Son are inseparably one in the place they have in Scripture, and ought to have in the heart of the believer, so the blessed Son and Spirit are inseparably one too. The more complete the surrender is to God for the teaching and power of the Spirit to reveal Christ in the heart, the more true and full will be the vision of the Son as our Redeemer and our Lord. And so, on the other hand, the more Christ Jesus becomes the all in all of the believer's heart and life, the more dependent will he be on the divine teaching of the Spirit to keep fresh and bright the living reality of that blessed Son whom it is his one work to reveal and glorify.

God sent forth his Son; God sent forth the Spirit of his Son into our hearts. Let our worship and love and work for Christ ever be in the power of the Spirit. And let every thought of Christ and every act of faith in him be in the assurance that from him we receive the Spirit to be in us as rivers of living water.

Chapter 35

In Travail

'My little children, of whom I travail in birth again until Christ be formed in you.'
Galatians 4:19

In the epistles of Paul the character of the teaching and of the teacher is inseparable. He has not only a message of truth from the God of love, he himself is a living message, and bears witness with the Holy Spirit to the grace and power of God that has wrought in him what he preaches to others. The whole of Christianity is marked by being entirely and intensely personal. It was thus with our Lord Jesus. He spoke of his relationship to their Father and of their communion one with another as one of intimate personal attachment. With his disciples Christ exercised his influence in the power of his strong personality, drawing them on to what they could not understand by the subtle influence of a superior affection. And so Christ sent Paul, not only to preach the

Gospel of the cross, but to live and act it out. It was this that moved him to write to the Thessalonians (1:5), 'Our gospel came unto you in power, and in the Holy Ghost, and in much assurance; as ye know what manner of men we were among you.' And later to the Corinthians (2 Cor 1:18) 'But as God is true, our word toward you was not yea and nay ... but in him was yea.' It is as this is understood and fully carried out in the life and practice of the messengers of the Word, that its divine power will make itself more manifest in the world. 'Ye are witnesses', our Lord Jesus said. 'The Spirit of truth ... he shall testify of me: And ye also shall bear witness because ye have been with me.' (John 15:26).

In the words of our text, Paul gives expression to the intense, motherly love with which he regards the Galatians as his little children, of whom he travails again in birth until Christ be formed again in them. We know what that word 'in travail' means. It is used of the anguish of a mother when, in the pangs of birth, she feels as if it would cost her her life to bring forth to birth the new life of the child she longs to see and embrace. Under the curse of sin the pain and anguish appear to be a necessity. By the grace of God they become the school for the exercise of that love which is ready to give its life for the life of another.

The prophet wrote of Christ, 'He shall see of the travail of his soul and be satisfied.' What that travail meant to him we know. As he drew near to the cross he spoke, 'I have a baptism to be baptized with; and how am I straitened till it be accomplished.' Not long after he said, 'Now is my soul troubled; and what shall I say? Father, save me from this hour: but for this cause came I unto this hour.' And so he moved on to the Garden, where he said: 'My soul is exceeding sorrowful unto death.' And in his sore soul travail appeared to him as if he could not possibly drink the cup and yield his life to the curse, until he had been strengthened from above to say, 'Thy will be done.' When he spoke the words on the cross, 'My God, my God, why hast thou forsaken me?'

the anguish had reached its uttermost, and he could say, 'It is finished.' And now he sees of the travail of his soul and is satisfied. And all who love him know no higher joy than to bring to him the souls for whom he died.

But is that travail really ended? 'It is Pascal who once said: 'Jesus will be in an agony till the end of the world. No sleep for him during this time!' This may be a mere conceit, but if the church of Christ is his body, and is the church of the Crucified, there seems to be ground for Pascal's words, and for the thought that the travail of the cross is not yet ended. What if Paul's words of filling up that which is lacking of the afflictions of Christ in my flesh for his body's sake (Col 1:24) require a larger meaning than we have yet given them.'

The power of God in the cross is a spiritual, divine energy that cannot cease working until the last redeemed soul is brought in. As little as men thought of that hidden energy, as it wrestled for them on the cross, do most Christians know or think about it. The power of the cross is a disposition which is not only to be found in Christ, but which works in all the elect souls who are ready wholly to yield themselves to its commands. As the crown of all the blessing the cross brings, there is an entrance into its deepest mystery – the mysteries of love. The mystery as seen in Christ of laying down his life and losing it entirely and absolutely for the sake of others, imparts itself to the soul, and the great work of intercession, with the service and the suffering to which it leads, is nothing less than the travail of the cross repeating itself. The life of Christ crucified is reproduced in us, and through us carries out its blessed purpose.

Christ had been all he could be during his life; it was only the travail of his soul in death that brought the great consummation. The church has, as far as she could, done something of work for him in the world. But will it not be as life from the dead when an increasing number of believers begin to see the travail of his soul is not ended yet and that, as the measure of this is fulfilled in us on behalf of the church that has yet to be gathered in, Christ will be able to do things through the church that he has never yet done?

'My little children, of whom I travail in birth again until Christ be formed in you.' Nothing less than the intense travail of soul that possessed the Apostle and was absolutely essential for winning some of these Galatian Christians to the true life of the Spirit is what the church in our day needs.

The Galatians believed in Christ, they trusted in him for the pardon of their sin. But they knew little of the power of the life of Christ formed within them. They understood not how complete their deliverance was from the law, and how divine the transition was to the life in the Spirit of God's Son that had been sent forth into their hearts. And are there not multitudes of Christians today who put their trust in Christ for the pardon of their sins, but know, oh, so little of their redemption unto the adoption of sons, and the fathers bestowment upon them of the Spirit of his Son as the only, the certain, the sufficient power for the life of a child of God.

Let us pray God fervently for teachers, whether in the pulpit or out of it, who can lead his children on to the knowledge of that indwelling Spirit, through whom Christ can be formed in them, teachers and believers, who travail of soul, give themselves up entirely to labour in prayer and service, to make known the riches of the glory of this mystery, Christ in you, the hope of glory.

Chapter 36

Flesh and Spirit

'Walk in the Spirit, and ye shall not fulfil the lust of the flesh. ... If ye are led of the Spirit, ye are not under the law.' Galatians 5:16,18

Let me remind the reader once again of the teaching that we have already had, to show us how the Holy Spirit takes entirely the place of the law, and gives complete deliverance from the power of the flesh. The sight of the crucified Christ led to the reception of the Spirit, for Christ redeemed us from the curse of the law that we might receive the Spirit through faith. Then, 'God sent forth his Son ... To redeem them that were under the law ... God hath sent forth the Spirit of his Son, crying Abba, Father.' The great object of the redemption of the cross was to deliver from the bondage of the law, and in its stead to give the liberty of the Spirit. In our text Paul gathers up all his argument in the simple but all-inclusive injunction: 'Walk in the Spirit, and ye shall not fulfil the lust of the flesh.' You can count upon it. What the law could not do to enable you to overcome the power of the flesh, the Holy Spirit will do most surely. If ye are led by the Spirit, ye are not under the law, but entirely and unceasingly free from it.

It needs time to realise the full scope of this teaching. To the Jew the law had dominion over his entire life and conduct, in his washing and dining, in his set times and seasons, everything was meant as a fulfilment of the law. The remark has been made by Christian visitors to India that nothing had struck them more than the way in which religion ruled the whole life of the heathen worshipper. If he had unintentionally profaned the laws of his caste, no sacrifice could be too great for him to make to have his restoration assured. Of the Muslim it has been said that the power of his religion consists not only in the faith in one God, but in the intensity of his belief that that one God ruled every moment and every action of his life, not for the will of his God. And it has been said by Christians that the Jews and the heathen make the Christian ashamed at the thought of how little in our Christian civilisation the power of God's law and God's will is heartily acknowledged in the ordinary course of daily life.

There can only be one reason for this. We do not understand that the tribute that the human mind in its darkness gives to the law of God is nothing less than a prophecy as to what the Spirit of God can do in the renewed man to enable him to live in the abiding joy of knowing and doing the will of his God. Oh, that we could take in the great thought that all the rule that the law was to exercise in Israel over the life and manners and worship of the nation, was to be but a faint shadow of that power over the flesh and its sin which the Spirit of God would exercise in the true believer. The redemption of the cross was not only in the justification of faith to secure our pardon. It was that, thank God, as an entrance into the new relation between the Father in heaven and the child whom Christ had redeemed. But it was also something more. It secured for us that indwelling Spirit through whom the law should be written in our heart, and become the very life of our being. The same God who sent his Son to redeem us on the cross, sent the Spirit of his Son into our heart to transform us into the likeness of that Son who had said, 'I come to do thy will, O my God.' That was indeed the true liberty of the Spirit. 'The Spirit of life in Christ Jesus hath made me free from the law of sin and death.' 'God sent his Son to condemn sin in the flesh, that the righteousness of the law might be fulfilled in us, who walk not after the flesh, but after the Spirit.' 'Walk by the Spirit, and ye shall not fulfil the lust of the flesh.'

We shall have occasion more than once to notice how confidently Paul speaks of his holy walk, his unclouded confidence in God's approval, his assurrance of being pleasing to God, and the entire absence of any allusion to the possibility of his not walking by the Spirit, or of his having given way to the flesh. There can be no question in Paul's life to us of greater moment than this. On it depends the confidence that what God has done for him he will do for us, as well as the urgency of the call for each of us to strive to find in the power of the Spirit what Paul teaches us to expect. Let the words sound in our ears, 'Walk by the Spirit, and ye shall not fulfil the lust of the flesh.'

The Galatians are a proof of how a church can have the Holy Spirit in its members and yet how feeble his workings may be. The contentions and hatred that existed were proof that the power of the Spirit was not known. And is not this the great lack in the church of our day? The power of the world in the church, its impotence to influence the masses around, its lack of consecration and self-sacrifice to carry the knowledge of Christ to every creature, the absence of that keen pursuit of holiness and love, and an all-pervading conformity to the image of the Son of God in human nature, show us that the Spirit is not present in that power in which he was promised. If we study the books written by our professors and preachers, even where the theology is sound in regard to the cardinal doctrines of the person and atoning work of our Lord, we shall find that the truth concerning the Holy Spirit is looked upon as a matter of course, without clear teaching that his power is essential to the true apprehension of Christ and his redemption. Many look for a revival from the preaching of reformation doctrine, and the cardinal truths of the deity, and the atonement of our Lord, and do not appear to see that it is possible to be zealous for these truths, while the power of the Holy Spirit is little sought and known. Surely in any revival that is to have power to raise the church out of its sickly state and to work effectually in establishing the kingdom of our Lord, all must be the work of the ever-blessed three in one. No less than the Father in his glory, and Christ in his redemption, must the Holy Spirit be known and honoured. It is in him alone that we have access through the Son to the Father.

And how is it that in churches where the Holy Spirit and God's Word are honoured one so seldom hears the testimony to the joy of walking in the Spirit and being so strengthened as not to fulfil the lust of the flesh. The answer is a simple but solemn one: It is a hard thing to yield one's self entirely to God the Holy Spirit; to cast out the divided life in which we have been accustomed; to follow Jesus unto his death, the absolute laying down of our life and giving up ourselves to the Holy Spirit as the fire of God's holiness; to walk unceasingly as Paul did, led by the Spirit. We have been so accustomed to the thought of the impossibility of our being led always and only and wholly by the Spirit, that it is difficult to form even a clear conception of how fully and surely the Spirit will take possession of a man. And when the preachers of the Word, the leaders of the flock, cannot sound a clear note in their testimony, no wonder that among the great majority of believers the thought of being filled with the Spirit is strange and hard. No wonder that one seldom hears a sermon on a text like this of Paul's, or hears the confession that in our life the victory of the Spirit over the flesh, as the permanent experience of a God-wrought deliverance, is experienced. Would that God might raise up men who have learned in secret what it is to live as crucified with Christ, so that he now lives in them, and the promise of Ephesians 3 becomes true, 'Filled with all the fulness of God.'

Do let us take the teachings of Paul in this epistle as to his crucifixion with Christ, and his no more living because Christ lived in him, as what is nothing less than is offered for daily use as the chief element of that liberty from law and from sin wherewith Christ has made us free.

Let us ask grace that we may fully accept this wonderful promise of a continual victory over the flesh in the pursuit of true holiness, and in our experience prove its truth and power: 'walk in the Spirit, and ye shall not fulfil the lust of the flesh.'

Chapter 37

The Crucifixion of the Flesh

'And they that are of Christ Jesus have crucified the flesh with the passions and the lusts thereof.' Galatians 3:24

This sentence comes very unexpectedly in the midst of the section on the Holy Spirit. It is preceded by what was said of the fruit of the Spirit, with the addition: 'against such as there is no law,' and is followed by the truth, 'If we live in the Spirit, let us also walk in the Spirit.' Here again we see how inseparably the cross and the Spirit are linked together. It reminds us of what we have already noticed in chapters 3 and 4. It was when Christ crucified was set before them that they received the Spirit by the hearing of faith. And, far more than this, it was when Christ redeemed us from the curse of the law that we could receive the promise of the Spirit through faith.

And, still further, it was when God sent forth his Son that he might redeem us from under the bondage of the law that God also sent forth the Spirit of his Son, by whom we could live in the life and the liberty of the children of God. It is through the cross that the Spirit came to us; it is through the preaching of the cross that we receive by faith the Spirit; it is through the redemption of the cross that we are freed from the law and receive the power of the Spirit in very deed to live the life of a child of God.

As we enter into the depth of this precious truth we shall see what a fullness of meaning there is in our text: 'They that are of Christ Jesus have crucified the flesh,' in its relation to what precedes and what follows about a life by the Spirit. To realise the command with its promise attached, 'Walk in the Spirit, and ye shall not fulfil the lust of the flesh,' we need to know the power by which the flesh can be conquered. They that are Christ's have crucified the flesh.

Note here first of all the perfect tense. It has been rightly said that, in all Paul teaches us of our participation in the crucifixion and death of Christ, the reference always is to a past and completed act. But it needs also to be said and to be accepted that what is implied in that past act must become a present reality in our daily experience. It was through the eternal Spirit that Christ offered himself to God on the cross; the power of the cross and the death of Christ is a living reality working in Christ's body here upon earth in the immediate and unceasing energy of the divine omnipotence. The cross is the great reservoir of divine power, and works out in every believer who fully yields himself all the disposition and mind of Christ in which he bore that cross. And so whether Paul says, 'I have been crucified with Christ,' or 'They that are Christ's have crucified the flesh,' or 'Knowing that our old man was crucified with him', or 'We died with Christ, we were made dead to the law by the body of Christ,' he is calling us to a life in which the cross and the death of Christ shall continually be made manifest in our mortal body. The perfect tense is carried on in an unceasing present.

Notice, too, how believers are spoken of as having done it themselves to crucify the flesh. The other texts speak of something that has been done to them. But here the power of the argument lies in the fact that they themselves have executed judgment on that vile thing in which there dwelleth no good. What can this mean in view of the impotence of the believer to do what God has himself already done in condemning sin in the flesh of Christ? And what in view of the thought that the great majority of believers have never seriously entertained the purpose or sought to carry it out? A little reflection will find the answer in our text.

'They that are Christ's have crucified the flesh.' It was with and in Christ that the crucifixion of the flesh was accomplished. Every believer, in yielding himself to Christ, yields himself to the crucified Christ. In doing so he accepts of all that Christ has been and done for him. Through ignorance his surrender to Christ meant far more than he knew. He gave in his adherence to what God had done in passing sentence of death on the flesh. As one who now belongs to Christ is taken hold of and owned by Christ, is united to Christ and shares with him the power of his death and resurrection, he has, if not expressly, then implicitly crucified the flesh. 'They that are Christ's have crucified the flesh.'

And here is now the great worth of this epistle and its teaching, that it brings believers to the knowledge and the consciousness of what faith in Christ truly means. Some simple man may have long been afraid of crossing the ocean. Some urgent need compels him at least to commit himself to the ocean steamer that is to carry him. He entrusts his life and his family and all he has to its keeping. And as the time goes on he finds out that the safety and the comfort, and all the provision made for his wants are something far beyond what he expected. He learns how to accommodate himself to a life of which he could form no conception before. It is thus with the

Christian, too. No one knows at first all that it means to bear the name given here – 'They that are Christ's.' But, if there only be a simple heart and a surrender to the teaching of God's Word, a Christian learns to understand how impossible it is to know and enjoy Christ aright, or to enter into the fullness of blessing and of fellowship that is waiting, without the whole-hearted acceptance of the message: 'They that are Christ's have crucified the flesh.' They were committed to it in believing; they were taught it as they yielded to the leading of the blessed Spirit: they have accepted it with their whole heart as one of the blessings of entire identification with their Lord. And the time comes that they will say with wonder, How was it that for so many years I never saw it that in this the very height of blessing is to be found, a full deliverance from the power of that accursed flesh that carried me so long into captivity. The cross now becomes the means of that closest and most perfect fellowship with my blessed Lord, in which I say, 'I have been crucified with Christ ... Christ liveth in me.' The cross and the Spirit are inseparably linked. The Spirit led Christ to the cross. The cross led to that wonderful giving of the Spirit by the Father to the Son, to be poured out on his body here upon earth. At Pentecost it was the preaching of the crucified Lord that led to the promise, 'Ye shall receive the Holy Spirit.' It is the Spirit that comes to the individual believer through the preaching of the cross. It is the Spirit that leads him to know himself as crucified with Christ, and it is by walking by the Spirit that the promise is fulfilled, 'Ye shall not fulfil the lusts of the flesh.' It is by the Spirit sealing our assurance that we belong wholly to the crucified Lord, that alone we are able every day to maintain our position of having crucified the flesh. It is through the Spirit that we learn to understand the Word. If we live by the Spirit, and count ourselves indeed to be Christ's, by the Spirit let us walk, and prove how the Spirit of life in Christ Jesus hath indeed made us free from the law of sin and death.

'They that are Christ's have crucified the flesh with its

affections and lusts.' In answer to the question that will come up a hundred times in the experience of a believer who is seeking to live this life, the words, 'They that are Christ's' will give the key. It was in Christ on the cross that his believing people were crucified with him. The closer the heart clings to him in abiding fellowship, the more perfect will be the desire for perfect conformity to his death, and the more surely will the faith, that reckons upon it that the full power of Christ's death is really ours, be imparted to us as we occupy ourselves with him. We shall begin to see that just what Christ needed we need. The Holy Spirit showed him that his death was an absolute necessity; there was no way out of his life in the flesh to the glory of God but through death. The Holy Spirit strengthened him and gave him the power to accept and consent to such a death at any cost. The Holy Spirit enabled him to give up the spirit into the Father's hand in the confident assurance that God would work in his utter impotence in the grave beyond all that men could hope or think. The blessed Spirit will work all this in us too as we abide in Christ. The insight that nothing less than a true and real death help us; the strong desire to be led by the Spirit to yield up all at any cost; the childlike faith that God, according to the working of the power of his might by which he raised Jesus from the dead, will indeed bring us through Christ's death into the new world and the new life and the new victory that he has opened up for us – for all this we can count upon the Spirit to work in us what he wrought in Christ. It is in this path that our text will unfold its meaning and its power; 'They that are Christ's have crucified the flesh with the affections and lusts.'

Chapter 38

Life and Walk

'If we live by the Spirit, by the Spirit let us also walk.' Galatians 5:25

Paul concludes his teaching on the Spirit by words in which he reminds us of the difference there may be beween a life by the Spirit and a walk by the Spirit, and the calling of the Christian to see that they are in perfect harmony. Life by the Spirit is God's gift. A walk by the Spirit is man's calling, made sure to him if he knows how to believe in and yield himself to the life of the Spirit which God has bestowed. Let us try to form a clear conception of the perfect and blessed harmony between the two.

Let us first remember the solemn truth that a man may be regenerate, truly born of God, and yet carnal. He may be truly in Christ, but, through lack of teaching, through lack of the Spirit's power in the ministry or the church in which he found the new birth, or through unbelief and disobedience may be still living and acting for the greater part under the power of the flesh. Such was the religion of the Galatians as Paul decribed it in connection with this passage, 'Ye bite and devour one another,' (5:15); 'Let us not be desirous of vain glory, provoking one another, envying one another,' (5:26). Alas, the sight is too often seen, a regenerate Christian acknowledging and counting himself a Christian, but carnal, walking after the flesh. He has no idea of the sin of such a state, very little desire for deliverance, and possibly when he hears the call, no faith that it is possible, either to himself or to God, to give him an entirely different life.

Look now at the other side; a man may be regenerate and also a spiritual man. He has been taught that the life within him is not only a power that the Holy Spirit has bestowed upon him, but that the Spirit has been given him as a teacher to open up to him the things of God, to reveal in his personal experience all that Jesus Christ lived in his life upon earth and worked out by his death. He understands that his whole life, every moment of it, and his whole walk are to be under the control and inspiration of the Holy Spirit. It is not enough to him to know that he lives by the Spirit, that he is a regenerate man. He has learnt that God in the Holy Spirit has come down to take entire possession of him, to have the mastery over his whole being, and has undertaken most graciously to renew him day by day in the likeness of Christ Jesus. He has learnt to believe that in answer to prayer the working of the Holy Spirit will be maintained without ceasing, and so his life consists in every day yielding himself to his blessed working. He believes in the Holy Spirit; he rejoices in the assurance that what step by step appears impossible with man is possible with God, through the power of the Holy Spirit who worketh in him. In humble adoration he knows himself a child of God who has received the Holy Spirit as his light and power for his daily life upon earth.

Just note how Paul in the verse that follows what we

have quoted (6:1) writes of a man who has been overtaken in any trespass, 'Ye which are spiritual, restore such a one in the spirit of meekness.' Just as in 1 Cor 2:15; 3:1–4 Paul contrasted the spiritual and the carnal so sharply, so here too he addresses the spiritual; he indicates what one of their great marks will be, the Christlike meekness that will give itself and labour to save the fallen. Then he adds, 'Bear ye one another's burdens, and so fulfil the law of Christ.' What a deeply suggestive expression! He had said in chapter 3, 'As many of you as have been baptized into Chrit have put on Christ.' Christ covers them, Christ is their head. Christ is now the law of their being. By faith in Christ they receive the Spirit; as the head moves and inspires action of every member of the body, so the Spirit enables them at every point to fulfil the law of Christ.

When once this is understood it will be found that this is no hard saying of Paul's, 'If we live by the Spirit, let us also walk in the Spirit.' Everything depends on our yielding to the blessed Spirit. He comes not to take away our power of will and action. On the contrary his mission is the very opposite. He comes as the gift of God's love with the gracious mission first of opening to us the treasures that are in Christ, and then as we desire and long for them, to impart the power to live them out. And all those treasures are comprised in one word, Christ himself. The Father sent him to show us a man living according to the will of God; a man giving up and losing his life that he might impart it to others; a man exalted to the throne of heaven with the power of giving his Spirit to reveal himself in us, and transforming us into his likeness. The Spirit reveals Christ not only above us and outside of us, but dwelling in our heart, actually becoming in our daily walk and conduct, the life of our life.

Paul saw that, though the Galatians had received the Spirit through faith, yet they had known little of what it meant. They had not accepted him as their divine teacher. They had not known how absolutely dependent the Christian is for his education as a child of God on the daily teaching of the Spirit. They were ignorant of his great work, so further to reveal Christ in them that they would have found in him liberty from the law, and with that from the power of the flesh. In his closing paragraph here (Galatians 5:16–26) he claims that their whole life was to be subject to his teaching, and assures them that then the flesh would be kept in actual subjection, and the fruit of the Spirit brought forth abundantly. In three simple statements he comprises the whole teaching of the Spirit in its bearing on the practical Christian life. 'Walk in the Spirit, and ye shall not fulfil the lust of the flesh.' 'If ye are led by the Spirit ye are not under the law.' 'If we live in the Spirit, let us also walk in the Spirit.' This is the liberty wherewith Christ has made us free.

Does not the feebleness of the Christian life now have the same case as we find among the Galatians? They sought to perfect in the flesh what had been begun in the Spirit, and to seek in vain in a religion, which made a fair show in the flesh, the power of godliness. As a consequence the flesh asserted its power and they were impotent to live the life of love and holiness to which they were called. Is not the great need of the church of our day that Paul's teaching should with boldness be proclaimed as the only healing of our sores? It is possible to believe in Christ and yet not to have the full experience of his saving and sanctifying power. It is because we do not know how utterly dependent we are upon the direct teaching of the Holy Spirit to make Christ a power and a reality in our daily life. When one reads some of the many sermons, orthodox and evangelical, that are being published, one feels how little the message sets before the believer the standard of a life led by the Spirit of God, with its power of victory over the flesh, and as the fruit of that, its power of victory over the souls that are to be brought out of darkness, and led on into the glorious liberty of the Sons of God.

Just as at the Reformation the blessed doctrine of justification by faith became in the life of Luther and the Reformers the power of God unto salvation, so the second half of Paul's teaching needs to be taught distinctly, and unceasingly, until believers know what the life and walk in the Spirit is to which they are called, and which God will delight to give them. At the Reformation the great truth of the promise of the Spirit by faith did not get equal attention with that of justification by faith. As the natural result men rested too much in the orthodoxy of scriptural doctrine, and the succeeding ages witnessed a terrible decline in the power of devotion and holiness. Let us pray God that he would raise up men to whom it is given to see what the church needs and to preach the redemption of cross in all the fullness of its meaning – the promise of the Spirit by faith as the only power for revealing Christ in a life and walk such as his was, and as the only strength for overcoming the world and establishing the kingdom of Christ.

We often hear the desire expressed for a true revival of religion, as the only power of the church for fulfilling its calling, either among the masses in Christian lands or among the millions of heathen still unevangelised. Let us remember that such a revival can only begin with individual believers who yield their lives wholeheartedly to the control of the Holy Spirit, that through their testimony and intercession God may show forth his mighty saving power.

Chapter 39

The Cross and the World

'But God forbid that I should glory, save in the cross of our Lord Jesus Christ, by whom the world is crucified unto me, and I unto the world.' Galatians 6:14

Hitherto we have had the contrast of the cross and the law. Paul had said he was dead to the law, because he was crucified with Christ. Christ redeemed us from the curse of the law, having become a curse for us upon the cross. Here we have the contrast of the cross and the world. He had said (1:4) 'Who gave himself for our sins, that he might deliver us from this present evil world.' He had spoken of the law and its bondage as of the weak and beggarly rudiments of a worldly religion (Gal 4:9; Col 2:20). He had spoken of those who desire to make a fair show in the flesh, and to glory in the flesh (6:12–13). And here he glories in the Cross, because through it the world has been crucified unto him, and he unto the world. So long as the church does not understand what deep and terrible meaning there is in the power of this world, its glorying in the cross will fail to produce the wonderful effect it had in Paul's life.

In the words our Lord spoke of the world and its enmity to himself and his church, he let the light of heaven fall upon the world in its true and unchangeable character. 'He said unto them, Ye are from beneath; I am from above: ye are of this world; I am not of this world' (John 8:23). 'The prince of this world cometh, and hath nothing in me' (John 14:30). 'If ye were of the world, the world would love his own; but because ye are not of this world, therefore the world hateth you' (John 15:19). 'The world hath hated them, because they are not of the world, even as I am not of the world' (John 17:14). 'My kingdom is not of this world: if my kingdom were of this world, then would my servants fight' (John 18:36). The cross is the revelation of the inmost nature of the world, and is a sign of how the world treats Christ and all that is truly of Christ. The cross is the mark of all in whom Christ dwells in power. It is the everlasting symbol of the relation between the true disciples of Christ and the world. The Apostle knows himself to be crucified to it, to have crucified it, and so ever to regard it as crucified to himself.

This crucifixion to the world is nothing less than a death to it. To all who confess that the world exercises its power upon them, to all who mourn that the root of all the impotence of the church is to be found in the worldliness that eats out the power of the spiritual life, the thought is a very solemn one, that nothing can deliver the Christian from it but an entire death to it, through the cross which crucifies us to the world. Many a Christian has at times prayed as he struggled with the power of sin in the heart. 'Oh, that God would strike it dead, this accursed evil nature.' And he thought there could not be any deliverance from it until the death of the body. He did not know that in the death of Christ, when he cried 'It is finished!' all his people received the assurance that his death carried theirs with it; they shared with him this crucifixion and death, and all the deliverance it brought.

When a believer sees and realises this he becomes willing to accept the truth. There is nothing but death can deliver me from the power of sin. And that not the death of my body, but the death of Christ revealing itself so in the body that the flesh, in which dwelleth no good thing, can be kept in the place of crucifixion and death. And what is true of death to the law, and death to sin, will be just as true of death to the world. To know and experience this will give a new meaning to Paul's outburst: 'God forbid that I should glory, save in the cross of our Lord Jesus Christ, by whom the world is crucified unto me.' To live as one of whom Christ said, 'Ye are not of the world,' one must be delivered from the spirit of the world, as Paul was delivered. We find no trace in any of his writings of the confession that the world was still too strong for him. The cross and its wonderful power was so real and so near, that he could day by day rejoice, 'God forbid that I should glory, save in the cross.' That means, not only the cross with its atonement, but the cross with its full redemption, proving itself in a life that ever breathes in the consciousness, I am crucified with Christ.

Just think a moment of how all nature teaches us that it is only through death that a higher state of existence can be reached and maintained. Think of the earth, exhausting itself, giving up its very life for the nourishment of the grass or hay it produces. Think again of how this grass again loses its life to reappear in the support of a still higher – the life of the sheep or ox that feeds on it. Think then of how this new life again sacrifices itself for the sake of the still higher life in man. And will it then be any wonder if man himself has to sacrifice the worldly life, the life under the secret, all-pervading influence of the world and its disposition, for that highest life in which Christ is all in all. Was it not even so with our blessed Lord himself in his life in the flesh? He, the holy, spotless One, had to give up his earthly life, in which he had borne our sin, that he might enter as man into the life and the glory of God. He had to die to sin that he might live unto God. Much more, surely, do we need to give up all that is of the world and its life ere we can live the true life of God in Christ Jesus. The deeper we enter into his death, the fuller the deliverance from sin.

If the church is to conquer the world, it must take the place that Paul does in this word. It must know and confess boldly that it is crucified and dead to the world. It must learn to glory in the cross just for this one reason, that it knows itself crucified to the world, and the world to it. The cross, as experienced in the daily life, must be its one glory, its distinguishing characteristic, to which its whole life bears witness. When the cross thus becomes its joy, it will find new meaning in the word, 'The joy of the Lord shall be your strength.' A church that is determined to know nothing but Jesus Christ and him crucified, will conquer the world.

Chapter 40

Paul Prays for Boldness

'Praying on my behalf, that utterance may be given unto me to make known with boldness the mystery of the gospel.' Ephesians 6.19

'Continue steadfastly in prayer, withal praying for us also, that God may open unto us a door for the word, to speak the mystery of Christ, that I may make it manifest as I ought to speak.' Colossians 4:2–4

When we pray for ministers and missionaries, our request is often very indefinite, with the chief thought of a blessing on their work in the hearers. We honour them as earnest, pious men, and long that God may make their work fruitful. This, however, is not what Paul thinks of in his request. He knows that when all is right with the preacher, and God's power and blessing rest on him, then the blessing will surely come. He therefore asks for prayer for himself both as what he preaches and how he preaches.

What he preaches

His one desire is that he might have grace to preach the mysteries of Christ. Or as he has it (Col 1:26,27): 'The riches of the mystery among the Gentiles; which is Christ in you, the hope of glory.' He was not content with preaching 'Christ for us': that was indeed the foundation, but he wanted the home and the life to be built on that foundation. That was the entrance, but the new life itself was nothing else than to have Christ living in us.

It was this that he testified of himself. 'Christ liveth in me'; 'Christ is our life'; 'For me to live is Christ.' As firmly as he believes in the incarnation and Christ crucified for us did he also believe in the Christ dwelling in the heart, in the being crucified with Christ, so that he no more lives, but Christ liveth in him. And it was this that he regarded as the great mystery he had to preach to the heathen. Until the believers were brought to understand and experience what it meant to have Christ dwelling in their hearts and revealed in their lives, he could not be satisfied.

And yet how little this is to be found in the church of our day. Paul's great prayer in which he asked for the Ephesian Christians that they might know what it is to have Christ dwell in the heart by faith, and so to know the love that passeth knowledge, and to be filled with all the fullness of God, is regarded by the most as a spiritual truth, far beyond the reach of the ordinary Christian. Dr McLaren said many years ago, in preaching on this text, that it was as if our modern church had entirely lost sight of this blessed truth. Men are content to trust in Christ for them on the Cross as their justification, and Christ for them on the Throne as their keeper and helper. But to have him in every day dwelling within them, controlling their whole being, and living out his life in them – this is more than can be asked of the ordinary Christian.

And yet we see how Paul speaks of it as the very centre truth of his preaching to the Gentiles, and how he asks for special prayer that he may be preserved from ever preaching anything less than the unsearchable riches of Christ, the riches of the glory of the mystery: Christ in you the hope of glory.

If we look back at the words of our Lord in John 17, is not this just what he prayed for: 'that they may be one, even as we are in them, and thou in me, that that the world may know that thou didst sent me, and lovedst them, even as thou lovedst me'? It is the person and the love of the living Christ, in his believing people, 'I in them,' that will persuade the world of the divine love dwelling in them even as Christ dwells in them.

How he preaches

'That I may speak boldly as I ought to speak.' The temptation was ever near to meet the wisdom of man in those to whom he spoke. We must remember that the Gentiles, or heathen, were not, as so many in our days are, savages in utter darkness. Egyptian and Babylonian, Grecian and Roman philosophy had trained men to think about unseen things. The whole spirit of the world tempted Christians to be content with the first elements of salvation, and not to press on to the life in which the world, with its wisdom and its pleasure, had to be entirely sacrificed ere Jesus Christ could take possession of the heart and rule the whole life. He had been preaching for twenty years, but he still felt the need of the help of continued intercession, that his dependence might be on God alone to speak as he ought to speak. In 1 Corinthians and 1 Thessalonians he tells how his speaking had been 'in demonstration of the Spirit and of power,' and how his Gospel 'came not in word only, but also in power, and the Holy Ghost, and in much assurance.' Oh, brethren, he cries, help me by your prayer that I may never preach otherwise! The fullness of an indwelling Christ, in the power of the Holy Spirit.

What a lesson for every minister and every missionary. Preach to your converts, Christ in you, the hope of glory. Preach as one who, like Paul, can say, 'Christ liveth in me. For me to live is Christ.' And as you preach, prove it in your life that the direct communion with Christ Jesus gives a life and a power that frees from the power of the world. Live as those who are prepared to sacrifice everything in the world that could keep them from knowing Jesus Christ intimately. Thus will you be able to lift up Jesus Christ, the Christ incarnate of Calvary, the Christ in you, the hope of glory.

And learn from Paul to take your people into your confidence. Tell them how you long to live, and what you desire above all to preach, and how you ask their help to wait on God that you may make the mystery manifest as you ought to speak. As you speak out of a heart and life in which Christ is felt, you and your people may be bound together in the bonds of Jesus Christ, and your and their prayer-life will bring down the blessing on which the Apostle counted so confidently when he wrote these words.

Chapter 41

Paul's Request for Prayer

'I beseech you, brethren, that ye strive together with me in your prayers to God for me; that I may be delivered from them that do not believe in Judaea; and may come to you with joy by the will of God.'
Romans 15:30–32

Paul had in the first chapter of Romans told them how he made mention always of them in his prayers, making request that he might have a prosperous journey by the will of God to come to them. He knew that he would see Rome, but as yet had no idea how he would get there. He intended first to visit Jerusalem, but knew not how he would be delivered from the dangers to which he might be exposed through his adversaries among the Jews. He asks them to strive together with him in prayer that he might be delivered from them who do not believe in Judaea. We know from the Acts through what dangers he had to pass. Men had vowed not to eat until they had killed him. Was it owing to the prayers of the saints in Rome to whom he writes that that deliverance came? Paul evidently felt confident that their prayers would not be in vain.

Baumgarten, in his Commentary on the Acts, has some most suggestive thoughts on this subject. He points out how the Roman Empire was utterly hostile to the Kingdom of Christ. We see it in our Lord's crucifixion, and later on in the death of James. We see signs of it in Paul's treatment at Philippi, and in Felix, willing to show the Jews a pleasure, leaving Paul bound for two years. Festus himself, willing to do the Jews a pleasure, offered to send Paul to Jerusalem. And all at once he allows Paul's appeal to Caesar, and the Roman Empire becomes responsible for Paul's deliverance from the Jews and his safe conduct to Rome.

'The question arises, has anything new happened that the world empire becomes the servant of Christ's Kingdom in bringing the Apostle to preach the Gospel in Rome itself! Something new has taken place. The conversion of the Gentiles has gathered large companies in many cities, and even in Rome itself. Of these communities we know with what devotion and love they regarded Paul, and accompanied him in wrestling prayer on his journey. This prayer of the saints, rendered effective by the Great High Priest in Heaven, is the power which has conquered the world power. The prayer of the saints, in close and living fellowship with their Head in Heaven, is the new power working on the earth. By the power of the Holy Spirit the saints knew that they had to battle with the powers of darkness, and yet were assured that in their living fellowship with the Lord in Heaven its power had been broken and overcome.'

Such thoughts give us an insight into what a reality there was in Paul's request for intercession, as a striving together with him in prayer, what actual power there was for effectual, much-availing prayer in the hearts of the saints, and what the victory was that had been won in heaven, and manifested on earth in God's servant. The lesson comes to us as from heaven that, if the Missionary would train his converts in the art of fervent prayer, he would have in them a mighty power to wield against the forces of darkness. The mighty power of Rome had to yield to the power of prayer.

See how Paul applies this faith in other circumstances. Just before writing the second epistle to the Corinthians he had in Asia 'been pressed out of measure, above strength, insomuch that we despaired even of life; But we had the sentence of death in ourselves. But God delivered us: in whom we trust that he will yet deliver us; ye also helping together by prayer for us.' Paul had such a vision of the spiritual unity of the body of Christ through all its members that he felt himself actually dependent upon the prayer of the churches. Where he stood alone he knew God as a God of prayer, and had power with him. But where he had believers to whom he was linked, he felt their prayer to be indispensable for his experience of God's power.

It is only when this sense of unity binds minister and people, binds all believers together, that the full power of the Holy Spirit can be expected to work. 'For the gift bestowed upon us by the means of many persons thanks may be given by many on our behalf,' an unceasing sacrifice of prayer and praise.

Just one more passage: In writing to the Philippians from Rome, he tells of 'Some indeed preach Christ even of envy and strife supposing to add affliction to my bonds.' He was content, he rejoiced and would rejoice because Christ was preached. 'For I know that this shall turn to my salvation through your prayer, and the supply of the Spirit of Jesus Christ.' Rome and Philippi were far asunder. But Paul lived so in prayer for the churches, and had taught them so to pray for him and his work, that he felt assured that every seeming evil would work out for his salvation, through their prayer and the consequent supply of the Spirit of Jesus Christ.

Let us pray for ministers and missionaries and workers, that the Holy Spirit may give us a new vision of the inconceivable power that prayer can exert. And many that vision lead to a new entrance upon the life of intercession, as the one great means of grace for the strengthening of the ministry and for the growth of believers in their holy calling as the priests of the most high.

The Africa Evangelical Fellowship

The AEF is an international evangelical mission. For more information about their work, please contact them at their International office, 17 Westcote Road, Reading, Berks RG3 2DL.

The AEF has hundreds of opportunities for both long and short term service in evangelism, church planting, education, medical administration, youth work and other practical fields.

Other AEF offices are:-

Australia
PO Box 292
Castle Hill
New South Wales 2154

Canada
470 McNicoll Avenue
Willowdale
Ontario M2H 2E1

USA
PO Box 2896
Boone
North Carolina 28607

United Kingdom
30 Lingfield Road
Wimbledon
London SW19 4PU

Zimbabwe
99 Gaydon Road
Graystone Park
Borrowdale
Harare

South Africa
Rowland House
6 Montrose Avenue
Claremont 7700

New Zealand
PO Box 1390
Invercargill

Europe
5 Rue de Meautry
94500 Champigny-sur-Marne
France